Identity Po
Brief Gu

By

Julian Henley

Other works by Julian Henley:

"The Anatomy of a Healthy Marriage"

"Debunking The Myth of Non-Binary Gender"

"Dickie A Cumming: The Prequel (Part I)" - anti-woke visual novel available to download at Steam Games

To Lauren

and

To Emma:

bastions of stability in an increasingly crazy world

Chapter 1: The Woke Revolution

The Origins of Wokeness

In the beginning, there was darkness. And then, there was wokeness. But where did this peculiar phenomenon come from? How did it infiltrate every aspect of our lives, from politics to pop culture? Well, my dear reader, let me take you on a journey back in time to uncover the origins of wokeness.

Some say that wokeness emerged from the depths of academia, where scholars with too much time on their hands pondered the mysteries of the universe. These intellectuals, armed with their fancy degrees and even fancier jargon, sought to deconstruct everything we hold dear. They questioned the very foundations of society and proclaimed themselves the arbiters of truth.

But it wasn't just the ivory towers of academia

that birthed wokeness. No, it spread like a virus through the corridors of power and influence. Politicians and activists saw an opportunity to gain power and control by dividing people into ever smaller and more oppressed groups. They preached the gospel of identity politics, where your worth as a human being is determined by your immutable characteristics.

And so, wokeness seeped into our culture like a toxic gas. It infected our schools, our workplaces, and even our entertainment. Suddenly, everything became about race, gender, and sexuality. No longer were we individuals with unique thoughts and experiences. We were reduced to mere representatives of our respective groups.

But why did wokeness catch on so quickly? Why did people embrace this ideology with such fervor? Well, my friend, I believe it has something to do with human nature. You see, we humans have a tendency to seek meaning and purpose in our lives. We want to feel like we're part of something bigger than ourselves.

And that's where wokeness comes in. It offers a sense of belonging, a sense of righteousness. By identifying as woke, you become a member of the enlightened few who have transcended the ignorance of the masses. You get to pat yourself on the back for being so morally superior.

But here's the thing: wokeness is not about equality or justice. It's about power and control. It's about silencing dissenting voices and enforcing conformity. It's about creating a hierarchy of victimhood where some groups are deemed more oppressed than others.

So, my dear reader, as we embark on this journey through the absurdities of wokeness, let us remember one thing: it's okay to question the status quo. It's okay to challenge the prevailing narratives. And most importantly, it's okay to think for ourselves. Because in a world gone mad with wokeness, critical thinking is our only salvation.

The Rise of Identity Politics

In the not-so-distant past, politics used to be about big ideas and grand visions for society. It was about economic policies, foreign relations, and the pursuit of liberty. But alas, those days are long gone. Today, politics has been reduced to a never-ending battle over identity.

Identity politics is the belief that one's identity - whether it be based on race, gender, sexuality, or any other characteristic - is the most important aspect of who they are. It's the idea that we should judge people not by the content of their character, but by the color of their skin or their gender identity.

Now, don't get me wrong. I understand the importance of recognizing and celebrating our differences. Diversity is a beautiful thing. But when we reduce people to nothing more than their identity labels, we lose sight of their individuality and humanity.

Identity politics has infiltrated every aspect of our lives. It's in our schools, our workplaces, and even our entertainment. We're constantly bombarded with messages telling us that our worth as individuals is determined solely by our identity group.

But what does this obsession with identity really achieve? Does it bring us closer together as a society? Does it solve the pressing issues of our time? No, it does not. In fact, it only serves to further divide us and perpetuate a victim mentality.

Identity politics is a dangerous game. It encourages us to view the world through a narrow lens, where everyone is either an oppressor or a victim. It stifles debate and discourages critical thinking. It tells us that our opinions and experiences are only valid if they align with the prevailing narrative.

But here's the thing: we are more than just our identities. We are complex individuals with unique thoughts, feelings, and experiences. Our worth should not be determined by the color of our skin or our gender identity, but by the content of our character.

So let's reject this divisive ideology and focus on what truly matters - our shared humanity. Let's have conversations based on ideas and principles, rather than identity labels. Let's celebrate our differences while recognizing that we are all part of the same human family.

In the end, it's not about who we are on the outside that defines us, but who we are on the inside. And that is something no identity label can ever capture.

The Language Police

In the ever-evolving world of wokeness, language has become a battleground. The Language Police, armed with their dictionaries and thesauruses, patrol the streets of discourse, ready to pounce on anyone who dares to utter an unapproved word or phrase.

Gone are the days when words were mere tools for communication. Now, they are weapons of mass destruction, capable of causing irreparable harm to fragile egos and delicate sensibilities. The Language Police have taken it upon themselves to protect us from the horrors of offensive language, but in doing so, they have created a linguistic minefield where one wrong step can lead to social annihilation.

The rules of engagement are constantly

changing. What was acceptable yesterday is now deemed offensive today. It's like trying to navigate a maze blindfolded while someone keeps moving the walls. One moment you're using a perfectly innocuous word, and the next moment you're being accused of hate speech.

Take the word trigger, for example. Once upon a time, it was a harmless term used to describe something that caused a strong emotional response. But now, it has been hijacked by the Language Police and turned into a weapon against free expression. If you dare to use the word trigger in any context other than discussing trauma, you risk being labeled insensitive and ignorant.

And let's not forget about the ever-expanding list of problematic words and phrases. It seems like every day, a new word is added to the forbidden lexicon. You can't say manhole anymore because it's not inclusive. You can't say freshman because it's not gender-neutral. You can't even say hey guys because it's not inclusive enough. The Language Police have become the arbiters of linguistic purity, and they won't rest until every word in the English language has been sanitized and stripped of any potential offense.

But here's the thing: language is fluid. It evolves over time, reflecting the changing values and attitudes of society. Trying to freeze language in a particular moment is like trying to stop a river from flowing. It's futile and ultimately counterproductive.

Instead of policing language, we should be focusing on fostering open and respectful dialogue. We should be teaching people how to engage in meaningful conversations, how to listen to different perspectives, and how to challenge ideas without resorting to personal attacks.

The Language Police may think they're protecting us from harm, but in reality, they're stifling creativity, inhibiting free thought, and creating a culture of fear and self-censorship. We need to reclaim our words and our voices from the clutches of linguistic tyranny. We need to embrace the messiness of language and celebrate its power to connect, inspire, and challenge.

So let's raise our voices and say it loud and clear (like *Mike & The Mechanics*): we will not be silenced by the Language Police. We will not be confined by their ever-changing rules. We will use our words to express ourselves, to question, to provoke, and to unite. Because in the end, it's not about the words we use; it's about the ideas behind them.

Cancel Culture and its Consequences

Ah, cancel culture. The modern-day equivalent of the Salem witch trials, where instead of dunking suspected witches in water to see if they float or sink, we simply dunk them on social media until their careers sink. It's a delightful pastime for the woke warriors of our time.

Cancel culture is the ultimate weapon in the arsenal of the perpetually offended. It's a way to silence anyone who dares to have a different opinion or make a mistake. And let's face it, we all make mistakes. But in the court of cancel culture, there is no room for forgiveness or redemption.

The consequences of cancel culture are far-reaching and deeply troubling. It creates an environment of fear and self-censorship, where people are afraid to speak their minds or express their true thoughts and feelings. It stifles creativity and innovation, as artists and writers tiptoe around sensitive topics for fear of being canceled.

But perhaps the most insidious consequence of cancel culture is its impact on intellectual discourse. In a healthy society, ideas should be debated and challenged. We should be able to engage in thoughtful discussions and learn from one another's perspectives. But cancel culture shuts down these conversations before they even have a chance to begin.

Instead of engaging with ideas we disagree with, we simply label them as problematic or offensive and move on. We create echo chambers where only our own views are heard and validated. And in doing so, we miss out on the opportunity for growth and understanding.

Cancel culture also undermines the principles of justice and due process. In the court of public opinion, there is no presumption of innocence. Accusations are enough to ruin someone's reputation and livelihood, without any evidence or fair trial. It's a dangerous precedent to set, and one that can have devastating consequences for individuals and society as a whole.

Now, I'm not saying that there aren't times when canceling someone is justified. There are certainly cases where individuals have engaged in truly abhorrent behavior and deserve to face consequences. But cancel culture has become a knee-jerk reaction to any perceived offense, no matter how minor or unintentional.

So what's the solution? How do we combat cancel culture without condoning harmful behavior? It starts with fostering a culture of empathy and understanding. Instead of immediately jumping to judgment and condemnation, we should strive to listen and learn from one another.

We should also encourage open dialogue and debate, even when it makes us uncomfortable.

It's through these conversations that we can challenge our own beliefs and grow as individuals. And if someone does make a mistake, we should be willing to offer forgiveness and a chance for redemption.

In the end, cancel culture is a symptom of a larger problem in our society – the inability to tolerate dissenting opinions or engage in civil discourse. If we want to move forward as a society, we must be willing to confront this problem head-on and embrace a culture of intellectual curiosity and open-mindedness.

So let's put down our virtual pitchforks and torches, and instead pick up the tools of empathy, understanding, and forgiveness. Only then can we truly progress towards a more inclusive and tolerant society.

The Hypocrisy of the Woke Elite

Ah, the woke elite. Those self-proclaimed champions of social justice and equality who love to lecture us mere mortals about our privilege and unconscious biases. They are the enlightened ones, the arbiters of what is right and wrong in this topsy-turvy world. But let me tell you, dear reader, their hypocrisy knows no bounds.

Take, for example, their love for all things organic and sustainable. They will proudly sip their fair-trade coffee from reusable cups while lecturing you about the evils of single-use plastics. But behind closed doors, they have no qualms about hopping on a private jet to attend a climate change conference in some exotic location. Oh, the irony!

And let's not forget their obsession with diversity and representation. They will shout from the rooftops about the need for more women and people of color in positions of power. But when it comes to their own organizations and institutions, they conveniently forget about diversity quotas and meritocracy. It's all about who you know and who can further their own agenda.

But perhaps the most glaring example of their hypocrisy is their disdain for capitalism. They will decry the evils of big corporations and wealth inequality while sipping on their Starbucks latte and scrolling through their iPhone. They conveniently forget that it is capitalism that has given them the luxury to sit around all day tweeting about social justice instead of working in a coal mine or plowing fields.

And let's not even get started on their love for censorship and cancel culture. They will preach about the importance of free speech and open dialogue, but the moment someone disagrees with them or says something they find offensive, they are quick to silence and shame them. It's a classic case of do as I say, not as I do.

But fear not, dear reader, for there is hope. The hypocrisy of the woke elite is so glaringly obvious that even the most ardent followers are starting to question their motives. People are waking up to the fact that these self-appointed guardians of morality are nothing more than power-hungry hypocrites.

So the next time you find yourself being lectured by a member of the woke elite, take a step back and ask yourself: do they practice what they preach? Are they truly committed to the ideals they espouse? Or are they just using their platform to further their own agenda and boost their own egos?

Remember, dear reader, true social justice and equality can only be achieved when we hold everyone accountable, including those who claim to be our moral superiors. Let us not be blinded by their virtue signaling and empty rhetoric. Let us demand consistency and integrity from those who seek to lead us down the path of wokeness.

Chapter 2: The Absurdity of Identity Politics

Intersectionality Gone Mad

Ah, intersectionality. The word itself sounds like a complicated mathematical equation that only a genius could solve. But fear not, dear reader, for I shall attempt to unravel this tangled web of identity politics for you.

Intersectionality is the belief that all forms of oppression are interconnected and that one's identity is shaped by multiple intersecting factors such as race, gender, sexuality, and so on. It's like a game of oppression bingo, where the more boxes you tick, the more oppressed you are.

Now, I must confess that I find this whole concept rather perplexing. It seems to me that intersectionality has taken a wrong turn somewhere along the way and ended up in a land of absurdity.

You see, according to the rules of intersectionality, certain identities are deemed more oppressed than others. For example, a black woman is considered more oppressed than a white woman because she has two boxes ticked instead of just one. It's like oppression Olympics, where everyone is vying for the gold medal in suffering.

But here's where things get really interesting. What happens when two oppressed identities collide? Let's say we have a disabled transgender person of color. According to the rules of intersectionality, this person should be the ultimate champion of oppression. They should be the voice that speaks for all the marginalized and oppressed. But alas, it's not that simple.

You see, in the world of intersectionality, there is a hierarchy of oppression. And in this hierarchy, some identities are more equal than others. So even though our disabled transgender person of color has three boxes ticked, they may still be overshadowed by someone who has four or five boxes ticked.

It's like a never-ending game of oppression one-upmanship. Who can be the most oppressed? Who can claim the highest position on the ladder of victimhood? It's a race to the bottom, where everyone is desperately trying to prove just how oppressed they are.

But let me ask you this: does this obsession with identity and victimhood really help anyone? Does it bring about real change or does it just create more division and resentment?

I fear that intersectionality has become a weapon to silence dissenting voices and stifle meaningful debate. It has turned us into a society where your worth is determined by your identity and where your opinions are dismissed based on your perceived level of privilege.

So let us not get caught up in this absurd game of intersectionality. Let us instead focus on what unites us as human beings – our shared values, our common goals, and our capacity for empathy and understanding.

For in the end, it is not our identities that define us, but our actions and our character. And it is through dialogue and open-mindedness that we can truly make progress and create a more inclusive and just society.

Now, I understand the importance of respecting people's identities and making them feel seen and heard. But when it comes to pronouns, things have gotten a little out of hand. It used to be simple. You were either a he or a she. But now we have an entire alphabet soup of pronouns to choose from. It's like ordering at a fancy restaurant where the menu is written in hieroglyphics.

First, we had the gender-neutral pronoun they. Fair enough. It's been around for centuries and has served us well. But then came the onslaught of new pronouns. Suddenly, we had ze, hir, xe, and even ey. I don't know about you, but I feel like I need a degree in linguistics just to have a conversation these days.

And let's not forget the ever-expanding list of prefixes and suffixes that people are attaching to their pronouns. We now have cis, trans, non-binary, genderqueer, and the list goes on. It's like playing a game of Scrabble where every word is worth a million points and you need a dictionary just to keep up.

But here's the thing: pronouns are supposed to make communication easier, not harder. They're meant to help us understand who we're talking about without having to resort to finger-pointing and wild gesticulations. But with this ever-expanding pronoun palette, it feels like we're back in the Tower of Babel, where everyone is speaking a different language and no one can understand each other.

And let's not forget the minefield of misgendering. One wrong pronoun and you're labeled a bigot faster than you can say linguistic sensitivity. It's like walking on eggshells, but instead of eggs, it's pronouns. And instead of shells, it's the fragile egos of those who take offense at the slightest linguistic misstep.

Now, don't get me wrong. I believe in treating people with respect and using the pronouns they prefer. But when we start policing language to the point where a simple slip of the tongue can ruin your reputation, we've gone too far. It's like living in a dystopian novel where Big Brother is watching your every word and Thought Police are ready to pounce on any linguistic transgressions.

So, my friends, let's take a step back and remember that language is a tool for communication, not a weapon for division. Let's find a way to respect people's identities without turning pronouns into a linguistic minefield. And most importantly, let's remember that behind every pronoun is a human being with thoughts, feelings, and a whole lot more to offer than just a label.

Cultural Appropriation or Appreciation?

Ah, cultural appropriation, the hot topic that has everyone in a tizzy. It seems that these days, you can't even breathe without someone accusing you of stealing their culture. I mean, come on people, can't we all just get along and share our cultural goodies like a bunch of civilized human beings? Apparently not. We live in a world where borrowing from another culture is seen as a crime worse than stealing candy from a baby. And let me tell you, the language police are out in full force, ready to pounce on anyone who dares to wear a sombrero on Cinco de Mayo or eat sushi without a Japanese passport.

Now, don't get me wrong, I understand the importance of respecting and appreciating different cultures. But when did we become so sensitive that we can't even enjoy a plate of pad thai without being accused of cultural theft? It's like we're living in some sort of dystopian nightmare where everyone is walking on eggshells, afraid to step out of their own cultural bubble for fear of offending someone.

But here's the thing: culture is meant to be shared. It's what makes us human. Throughout history, cultures have borrowed from each other, exchanged ideas, and created something new and beautiful. Take music, for example. Jazz wouldn't exist without African rhythms and European harmonies coming together in perfect harmony. And let's not forget about food. Can you imagine a world without fusion cuisine? I shudder at the thought.

But according to the cultural appropriation police, if you're not born into a certain culture, you have no right to partake in its traditions.

Sorry, but that's just plain ridiculous. Last time I checked, culture wasn't a members-only club with a strict dress code and secret handshake. It's a living, breathing thing that evolves and adapts over time. And guess what? It's meant to be shared with the world.

Now, I'm not saying that cultural appropriation doesn't exist. There are certainly instances where it can be disrespectful or offensive. But let's not throw the baby out with the bathwater here. We need to distinguish between cultural appreciation and cultural appropriation. Appreciation is about learning, respecting, and celebrating another culture. It's about understanding the history and significance behind certain traditions and embracing them in a way that shows genuine interest and respect.

On the other hand, appropriation is about taking elements of a culture without understanding or respecting their meaning. It's about using someone else's culture as a fashion statement or a trend without acknowledging its roots or giving credit where credit is due. And yes, that can be problematic.

But instead of jumping down each other's throats every time someone wears a bindi or gets a henna tattoo, maybe we should focus on educating ourselves and having open, respectful conversations about cultural exchange. Let's celebrate the beauty of diversity and learn from each other instead of building walls around our own cultures.

So next time you see someone rocking a kimono or grooving to reggae music, take a moment to appreciate the fact that we live in a world where cultures can come together and create something truly magical. And if you're still worried about cultural appropriation, just remember this: imitation is the sincerest form of flattery. So let's flatter each other to death and create a world where cultural exchange is celebrated, not condemned.

The Dangers of Virtue Signaling

Ah, virtue signaling. The noble art of publicly proclaiming your moral superiority without actually doing anything useful. It's like a modern-day version of the Emperor's New Clothes, where everyone pretends to see the emperor's fabulous outfit even though he's standing there butt naked. Only in this case, it's not just the emperor who's deluded, it's the whole damn kingdom.

Virtue signaling has become the currency of the woke elite. It's their way of showing off how enlightened and progressive they are without having to lift a finger or actually make any meaningful change in the world. They'll post a black square on Instagram to show their support for racial justice, but when it comes to actually addressing systemic racism or advocating for policy reform, they're nowhere to be found.

But hey, at least they got those likes and retweets, right? I mean, who needs real action when you can just bask in the warm glow of virtual applause? It's like getting a participation trophy for being a good person without actually having to do anything good.

And let's not forget the performative allyship. You know, when someone from a privileged group jumps on the bandwagon of a marginalized cause just to boost their own social standing. They'll wear a safety pin to show they're an ally to the LGBTQ+ community, but when it comes to actually challenging homophobic attitudes or advocating for LGBTQ+

rights, they're nowhere to be found.

It's like they're playing a game of social justice dress-up, where they get to try on different causes and identities for a day and then go back to their privileged lives. It's all about appearances, not substance. They want the world to see them as virtuous and enlightened, but they don't actually want to put in the work or make any sacrifices.

But here's the thing about virtue signaling: it's not just harmless posturing. It can actually be detrimental to real progress. When people are more concerned with looking good than doing good, it creates a culture of superficiality and empty gestures. It allows people to pat themselves on the back for their supposed moral superiority without ever having to confront their own biases or challenge the status quo.

And let's not forget the chilling effect it can have on free speech. When people are more interested in being politically correct than engaging in honest and open dialogue, it stifles debate and prevents us from truly understanding each other. It's like we're all walking on eggshells, afraid to say the wrong thing and be labeled a bigot or a racist or whatever the woke word of the day is.

So let's call a spade a spade. Virtue signaling is not activism. It's not progress. It's just empty posturing and self-congratulation. If you really want to make a difference, put down your phone, step away from the keyboard, and actually do something. Get involved in your community, educate yourself on the issues, and use your voice to advocate for real change.

Because at the end of the day, actions speak louder than hashtags.

When Political Correctness Goes Wrong

Ah, political correctness. The gift that keeps on giving. Or should I say, the curse that keeps on cursing? Yes, my dear reader, political correctness is like that annoying relative who insists on correcting your grammar at every family gathering. You know the one I'm talking about. The one who thinks they're doing you a favor by pointing out that you used the wrong form of their in your Facebook post. Thanks, Aunt Mildred. I'll be sure to consult you for all my grammatical needs.

But I digress. Political correctness has infiltrated every aspect of our lives, from the way we speak to the way we think. It's like a virus that infects our brains and turns us into mindless drones, afraid to utter a single word for fear of offending someone. Heaven forbid we should express an opinion that goes against the prevailing narrative!

Take, for example, the case of poor Professor Smith. One day, Professor Smith innocently mentioned in class that he believed in meritocracy. Oh boy, did he step in it! The students were outraged. How dare he suggest that people should be rewarded based on their abilities and hard work? That's so...unfair! They demanded that Professor Smith be fired immediately for his offensive views.

Now, you might be thinking, But isn't meritocracy a good thing? Shouldn't we reward people based on their abilities? Ah, my naive friend, you clearly haven't been paying attention. In the world of political correctness, meritocracy is a dirty word. It's seen as a tool of oppression, a way to keep marginalized groups down. Apparently, we should all be given participation trophies just for showing up. Because nothing says equality like rewarding mediocrity.

But it's not just in academia where political correctness rears its ugly head. It's everywhere. In the workplace, you have to walk on eggshells for fear of offending your co-workers. God forbid you should make a harmless joke or express an opinion that doesn't align with the company's diversity and inclusion policy. You might as well kiss that promotion goodbye.

And let's not forget about social media. One wrong tweet or Facebook post and your life could be ruined forever. Just ask poor Sally Johnson, who made the mistake of expressing her support for a controversial political figure. Within minutes, she was bombarded with hate messages and death threats. Her employer promptly fired her to avoid any association with her offensive views.

But here's the thing about political correctness: it stifles debate and hinders progress. When we're afraid to speak our minds, we lose the opportunity to engage in meaningful dialogue and challenge each other's ideas. We become trapped in an echo chamber where only one perspective is allowed.

So what's the solution? Do we abandon political correctness altogether? Well, that might be a bit extreme. After all, we don't want to go back to the days of blatant racism and sexism. But we do need to find a balance. We need to create a culture where people feel comfortable expressing their opinions without fear of retribution.

And most importantly, we need to remember that words are just words. They only have power if we give them power. So let's stop being so easily offended and start focusing on the things that truly matter. Like Aunt Mildred's obsession with grammar. Now that's a battle worth fighting.

Chapter 3: The Silencing of Free Speech

Safe Spaces and Trigger Warnings

Ah, safe spaces and trigger warnings. The twin pillars of the woke revolution. These concepts are like the training wheels of adulthood, designed to protect fragile minds from the harsh realities of the world. It's as if we've regressed back to kindergarten, where everyone gets a participation trophy and no one's feelings can ever be hurt.

Safe spaces are these magical places where people can retreat to when they feel uncomfortable or triggered by something. It's like a little bubble where they can shield themselves from any ideas or opinions that might challenge their delicate sensibilities. It's a bit like living in a perpetual hugbox, where everyone agrees with you and no one ever says anything that might make you question your beliefs.

And then there are trigger warnings. These are little disclaimers that come before any potentially offensive or upsetting content. It's like a flashing neon sign saying Danger! Danger! This might hurt your feelings! Because apparently, we've reached a point where people need to be warned about the existence of ideas or opinions that might challenge their worldview.

Now, I understand that there are certain topics that can be genuinely triggering for some people. Trauma is a real thing, and it's important to be sensitive to those who have experienced it. But the problem with trigger warnings and safe spaces is that they've been taken to absurd extremes.

I mean, imagine if we applied this logic to every aspect of life. Warning: This movie contains scenes of violence. Please proceed with caution. Caution: This book contains ideas that might challenge your beliefs. Read at your own risk. Attention: This restaurant serves food that might not align with your dietary preferences. Enter at your own peril.

It's like we're trying to create a world where no one ever has to confront anything they find uncomfortable or offensive. But here's the thing: life is uncomfortable and offensive sometimes. It's messy and complicated and full of ideas and opinions that might make you uncomfortable. And that's okay.

The real world doesn't come with trigger warnings or safe spaces. It's a place where you have to learn how to navigate difficult conversations and confront challenging ideas. It's a place where you have to develop resilience and the ability to think critically.

But instead of preparing young minds for the real world, we're coddling them and shielding them from anything that might make them uncomfortable. We're creating a generation of fragile snowflakes who can't handle the slightest bit of adversity.

So here's a radical idea: instead of retreating to safe spaces and demanding trigger warnings, why not embrace discomfort? Why not engage with ideas that challenge your beliefs? Why not develop the resilience and critical thinking skills necessary to navigate the complexities of the real world?

Because let's face it, life isn't always going to be a safe space. And if we continue down this path of shielding ourselves from anything that might make us uncomfortable, we're going to end up living in a world where free speech is silenced and intellectual diversity is nonexistent.

Censorship in the Digital Age

Ah, the digital age. A time of endless possibilities, where information flows freely and ideas can be shared with the click of a button. Or so we thought. Little did we know that this brave new world would also bring with it a new form of censorship, one that would make even the most zealous book-burner blush.

In the good old days, if you wanted to censor someone, you had to go through the trouble of burning their books or banning their speeches. It was a lot of effort, and frankly, it just wasn't very efficient. But thanks to the wonders of technology, we now have a much more streamlined way of silencing dissenting voices - social media.

Yes, my friends, social media has become the modern-day equivalent of the town square, where ideas are exchanged and debates are held. But unlike the town square of old, this digital version comes with its own set of rules and regulations. And let me tell you, these rules are about as fair and balanced as a fox guarding a henhouse.

You see, social media platforms like Facebook and Twitter have taken it upon themselves to be the arbiters of truth and morality. They have appointed themselves as the guardians of public discourse, deciding what is acceptable speech and what is not. And let me tell you, they are not very good at it.

Take, for example, the case of poor old Aunt Mildred. Aunt Mildred is a sweet old lady who loves to share pictures of her cats and post inspirational quotes. But one day, she made the grave mistake of sharing a meme that was deemed offensive by the social media gods. And just like that, her account was suspended, her voice silenced.

Now, you might be thinking, Well, maybe Aunt Mildred deserved it. Maybe she really did cross the line. But here's the thing - the line keeps moving. What was acceptable yesterday is offensive today. What was funny last week is hate speech this week. It's like trying to hit a moving target blindfolded.

And it's not just Aunt Mildred who's feeling the wrath of the digital censors. It seems like every day there's a new story of someone being banned or deplatformed for expressing an unpopular opinion. Whether it's a comedian making a joke that some people find offensive or a journalist reporting on a controversial topic, no one is safe from the long arm of social media justice.

But here's the real kicker - these social media platforms claim to be bastions of free speech and open dialogue. They tout themselves as champions of democracy and defenders of the First Amendment. But when push comes to shove, they are more than happy to silence anyone who dares to challenge their worldview.

So what can we do in this age of digital censorship? Well, for starters, we can start questioning the authority of these social media giants. We can demand transparency and accountability. We can push back against the notion that a handful of tech billionaires should have the power to decide what we can and cannot say.

And most importantly, we can remember that free speech is not just a right, it's a responsibility. It's our duty as citizens of the digital age to speak up and speak out, even when it's uncomfortable or unpopular. Because if we don't, we risk losing the very essence of what makes us human - our ability to think, to question, and to challenge the status quo.

So let's not let the digital censors have the last laugh. Let's reclaim our voices and fight for a world where ideas are free to be shared and debated. And if all else fails, we can always go back to good old-fashioned book burning. At least then we'll have something warm to keep us company on those cold winter nights.

The Weaponization of Social Media

Ah, social media. The great equalizer. The platform that was supposed to give everyone a voice and connect us all in a global community. Well, that's what they told us anyway. But little did we know that this seemingly innocent tool would become a weapon of mass destruction in the hands of the woke brigade.

You see, social media was meant to be a place where we could share our thoughts, ideas, and cat videos with the world. But now it has become a battleground for the woke warriors to silence anyone who dares to disagree with their narrow-minded ideology.

It all starts innocently enough. You log onto your favorite social media platform and scroll through your feed. You see a post that catches your eye —a well-reasoned argument against some woke nonsense. You think to yourself, Finally, someone speaking some sense! So you decide to leave a comment expressing your support.

But little did you know that by doing so, you have just painted a target on your back. The woke warriors are always on the lookout for dissenting voices, ready to pounce on anyone who dares to challenge their fragile worldview.

Within minutes, your comment is bombarded with angry replies. The woke brigade has mobilized, and they are out for blood. They accuse you of being a bigot, a racist, a sexist, and any other -ist or -phobe they can think of. They don't bother to engage with your argument or provide any evidence to support their claims. No, they prefer to resort to name-calling and ad hominem attacks.

But it doesn't stop there. Oh no, the woke warriors have a whole arsenal of weapons at their disposal. They will screenshot your comment and share it with their followers, encouraging them to report you for hate speech or harassment. And before you know it, your account is suspended or even permanently banned.

But wait, there's more! The woke warriors will also dox you—publishing your personal information online for all to see. They will contact your employer, your friends, and your family, accusing you of being a dangerous extremist. They will stop at nothing to destroy your reputation and silence your dissenting voice.

And what's even more insidious is that social media platforms themselves have become complicit in this silencing of free speech. They claim to be champions of free expression, but in reality, they are nothing more than puppets in the hands of the woke elite.

They will shadowban users who dare to challenge the woke narrative—limiting the reach of their posts and hiding them from public view. They will manipulate algorithms to promote certain viewpoints while suppressing others. And they will bow down to the demands of the woke warriors, removing any content that they deem offensive or problematic.

So, my friends, be careful what you say on social media. The woke warriors are watching, and they will not hesitate to use every dirty trick in the book to silence you. But fear not, for the truth will always prevail. We must continue to speak out against the absurdities of identity politics, no matter the consequences. After all, if we don't stand up for free speech, who will?

Thought Police on Campus

Ah, the hallowed halls of academia, where free thought and intellectual exploration are supposed to reign supreme. Or at least that's what they used to be. Nowadays, universities have become breeding grounds for a new kind of species - the thought police.

These self-appointed guardians of political correctness patrol the campuses with their metaphorical batons, ready to strike down anyone who dares to utter an opinion that doesn't align with their narrow worldview. They claim to be fighting for social justice and equality, but in reality, they're just stifling debate and creating an echo chamber of conformity.

Imagine this scenario: you're sitting in a lecture hall, listening to a guest speaker who holds a different perspective than the prevailing ideology on campus. Suddenly, a group of students rise from their seats and start chanting slogans like No platform for hate speech! and Your words are violence! It's like a scene from a dystopian novel, except it's happening right in front of your eyes.

These thought police believe that they have the moral high ground and that their cause is so righteous that any dissenting opinion must be silenced. They've turned universities into intellectual battlegrounds where ideas are not debated but rather shouted down and suppressed.

But here's the thing - universities are supposed to be places where ideas are challenged and debated. They're supposed to be spaces where students can explore different perspectives and learn how to think critically. By shutting down opposing viewpoints, the thought police are doing a disservice to the very purpose of higher education.

And let's not forget about the professors who have fallen victim to the thought police. These brave souls, who dare to question the prevailing orthodoxy, are often subjected to public shaming campaigns and even threats of violence. It's a sad state of affairs when academics are afraid to speak their minds for fear of retribution.

The thought police claim that they're creating safe spaces for marginalized groups, but in reality, they're creating an environment of intellectual stagnation. How can we expect progress and innovation if we're not willing to engage with ideas that challenge our own?

It's time for universities to reclaim their role as bastions of free speech and open inquiry. We need to foster an environment where all ideas can be heard and debated, no matter how uncomfortable they may be. Only then can we truly expand our understanding of the world and move towards a more enlightened society.

So let's stand up against the thought police and reclaim our right to free expression. Let's embrace the messy, chaotic, and sometimes uncomfortable process of intellectual exploration Because in the end, it's through open dialogue and debate that we can truly grow as individuals and as a society.

How Political Correctness Stifles Debate

Ah, political correctness. The bane of free speech and the destroyer of lively debates. It's like a wet blanket that smothers any hint of dissent or disagreement. In the name of inclusivity and sensitivity, we've created a world where everyone tiptoes around each other, afraid to say anything remotely controversial. It's like walking on eggshells, but instead of eggs, it's fragile egos.

You see, in the world of political correctness, there are certain topics that are off-limits. You can't question certain ideas or challenge certain beliefs without being labeled a bigot or a hater. It's as if we've traded intellectual curiosity for intellectual conformity. And let me tell you, my friend, that is a dangerous trade indeed.

Take the issue of immigration, for example. It's a complex issue with many different perspectives and valid arguments on both sides. But in the world of political correctness, there is only one acceptable opinion: open borders and unlimited immigration. If you dare to suggest otherwise, you're immediately branded a racist or a xenophobe.

And it's not just immigration. It's a whole range of topics, from gender and sexuality to race and religion. If you deviate even slightly from the approved narrative, you're labeled a heretic and banished from the realm of polite society. It's like we're living in a modern-day Inquisition, where the thought police patrol the streets, ready to pounce on anyone who dares to speak their mind.

But here's the thing: stifling debate doesn't make us more tolerant or inclusive. It just creates an echo chamber where everyone agrees with each other and no one is challenged. And let me tell you, my friend, that is a recipe for intellectual stagnation.

You see, debate is how we grow as individuals and as a society. It's how we test our ideas and refine our arguments. Without it, we become stagnant and complacent. We stop questioning the status quo and start accepting things at face value. And that, my friend, is a dangerous path to walk.

So let's reclaim free speech from the clutches of political correctness. Let's have open and honest debates about the issues that matter to us. Let's challenge each other's ideas and beliefs without fear of being labeled a bigot or a hater. Let's embrace the messy, uncomfortable, and sometimes downright offensive world of free speech.

Because here's the thing: true progress doesn't come from silencing dissent. It comes from engaging with it, wrestling with it, and ultimately finding common ground. So let's put an end to the stifling grip of political correctness and let the free exchange of ideas flourish once again.

Chapter 4: The War on Comedy

Comedy in the Crosshairs

Ah, comedy. The art of making people laugh, of poking fun at the absurdities of life, and of providing a much-needed escape from the daily grind. But alas, in this woke world we find ourselves in, even comedy is not safe from the clutches of political correctness.

Gone are the days when comedians could freely crack jokes about anything and everything without fear of being canceled. Now, they must tiptoe around sensitive topics and carefully navigate the minefield of potential offense. It's like trying to perform stand-up comedy while wearing clown shoes on a tightrope.

In this brave new world, it seems that every joke has the potential to offend someone. And heaven forbid if you offend someone these days. You might as well pack up your comedy career and start selling insurance.

Comedians are now expected to be mind readers, to know exactly what will trigger each and every individual in their audience. It's like playing a game of Russian roulette with punchlines instead of bullets.

Satire, that glorious art form that uses humor to expose the follies and vices of society, is also under attack. The woke brigade has deemed satire to be too dangerous, too offensive, and too likely to hurt someone's feelings.

But here's the thing about satire: it's supposed to be biting. It's supposed to make you uncomfortable. It's supposed to challenge your beliefs and make you think. If it doesn't do that, then it's just a bad joke.

In this woke world, we seem to have forgotten how to laugh at ourselves. We take everything so seriously, so personally. We've lost the ability to see the humor in our own flaws and foibles.

But here's a little secret: laughing at ourselves is liberating. It allows us to acknowledge our imperfections and embrace our humanity. It reminds us that we're all in this crazy world together, stumbling and bumbling our way through life.

So how do we find humor in a world that seems determined to suck all the fun out of everything? Well, my friends, it requires a little bit of rebellion.

We must resist the urge to be offended by every little joke. We must reclaim our sense of humor and refuse to let it be stifled by the language police. We must laugh in the face of political correctness and embrace the joy that comes from a well-timed punchline.

Because at the end of the day, laughter is a powerful weapon. It has the ability to unite us, to break down barriers, and to remind us of our shared humanity. So let's not let the woke warriors take that away from us.

When Jokes Become Offense

Ah, comedy. The art of making people laugh, of bringing joy and mirth to the masses. Or at least it used to be. In this brave new world of wokeness, comedy has become a minefield of offense and hurt feelings. It seems that no joke is safe from the wrath of the perpetually offended.

Once upon a time, comedians were revered as the court jesters of society. They were the ones who could say the unsayable, who could poke fun at the powerful and challenge societal norms. But now, they are walking on eggshells, afraid that one wrong word or misplaced punchline will lead to their cancellation.

Take poor Dave Chappelle for example. A comedic genius who dared to tackle sensitive topics like race and gender with his razor-sharp wit. But oh no, he went too far for the woke brigade. They couldn't handle his jokes about transgender people or his refusal to bow down to their demands for political correctness.

And let's not forget about poor Kevin Hart. He was all set to host the Oscars, a dream come true for any comedian. But then some old tweets resurfaced where he made jokes about homosexuality. The outrage was swift and merciless. How dare he make jokes about a marginalized group? Never mind that comedy has always been about pushing boundaries and challenging societal norms.

It seems that in this woke world, there is no room for nuance or context. A joke is either offensive or it's not. There's no in-between. And if you dare to defend a comedian's right to make jokes, well, you must be a bigot or a misogynist or some other -ist or -phobe.

But here's the thing: comedy is supposed to be offensive. It's supposed to challenge our preconceived notions and make us uncomfortable. It's supposed to push boundaries and make us think. If we start censoring comedians and dictating what they can and cannot say, then we are killing the very essence of comedy.

And let's not forget that comedy is subjective. What offends one person may not offend another. We all have different senses of humor, and that's okay. Just because a joke doesn't make you laugh doesn't mean it should be banned from existence.

So let's stop this war on comedy. Let's allow comedians to do what they do best: make us laugh. And if a joke offends you, well, here's a radical idea: don't laugh. But don't try to silence those who find it funny. Because in the end, laughter is what brings us together, even in this divided and woke world.

The Decline of Satire

Ah, satire! That delightful art form that has been entertaining and enlightening us for centuries. From the biting wit of Jonathan Swift to the sharp social commentary of Mark Twain, satire has always been a powerful tool for exposing the follies and absurdities of society. But alas, in this woke world we find ourselves in, satire is under attack.

You see, dear reader, satire relies on exaggeration and irony to make its point. It takes reality and twists it just enough to make us laugh and think. But in this age of hypersensitivity and political correctness, satire is often misunderstood and misinterpreted.

Take for example the case of poor Mr. Johnathan Swift. Mr. Swift was a talented satirist who wrote a brilliant piece mocking the absurdity of identity politics. He created a fictional character named Sir Reginald Wokeington III, a pompous social justice warrior who took offense at everything and anything.

Now, you would think that readers would recognize Sir Reginald as a caricature, a larger-than-life figure meant to highlight the ridiculousness of extreme political correctness. But oh no! Instead, people took offense at the character and accused Mr. Swift of perpetuating harmful stereotypes.

It seems that in this woke world, satire is no longer allowed to be satire. It must be taken literally and analyzed for any potential harm it may cause. But where does this leave us, dear reader? Are we to abandon satire altogether and resign ourselves to a world devoid of laughter and critical thinking?

I say no! We must fight for the preservation of satire, for it is a vital part of our cultural heritage. Satire allows us to question authority, challenge the status quo, and expose hypocrisy. It is a powerful weapon against tyranny and oppression.

But how do we navigate this treacherous landscape? How do we ensure that our satirical works are not misunderstood or misinterpreted?

First and foremost, we must educate ourselves and others about the nature of satire. We must teach people that satire is not meant to be taken literally, but rather as a form of commentary and critique. We must encourage critical thinking and open dialogue.

Secondly, we must not shy away from controversy. Satire has always been provocative and boundary-pushing. It challenges our preconceived notions and forces us to confront uncomfortable truths. We cannot let fear of backlash or accusations of insensitivity silence us.

Lastly, we must remember that laughter is a powerful force for change. Satire has the ability to unite people through shared laughter and common understanding. It can bridge divides and break down barriers.

So let us not mourn the decline of satire, but rather let us rise up and defend it. Let us use our voices and our pens to create satirical works that challenge the absurdities of our world. Let us laugh at ourselves and find humor in the madness.

For as long as there are injustices to be exposed and hypocrisies to be ridiculed, satire will never truly die. It may be under attack, but it will always find a way to survive and thrive.

Laughing at Ourselves - A Lost Art?

Ah, laughter! The sweet sound that brings joy to our hearts and tears to our eyes. But in this woke world we find ourselves in, laughter is becoming a dangerous act. Yes, my dear reader, the art of laughing at ourselves has become a lost art. We are now expected to take everything so seriously that even a chuckle can be seen as an act of aggression.

Gone are the days when we could poke fun at our own foibles and laugh at the absurdities of life. No, now we must walk on eggshells and tiptoe around any topic that might offend someone's delicate sensibilities. Heaven forbid we should make a joke about race, gender, or any other identity category. That would be a cardinal sin in the church of wokeness.

But let me ask you this, dear reader: what is the purpose of comedy if not to hold up a mirror to society and make us laugh at ourselves? Comedy has always been a way for us to navigate the complexities of life and find common ground through shared laughter. It is a powerful tool that can bridge divides and bring people together.

Yet in this woke world, comedy is under attack. Comedians are being canceled left and right for daring to make a joke that might offend someone. They are accused of being insensitive, offensive, and even promoting hate speech. But let me tell you, my dear reader, comedy is not hate speech. It is an art form that requires skill, timing, and a deep understanding of human nature.

Now, I'm not saying that all jokes are created equal. There are certainly jokes that cross the line and perpetuate harmful stereotypes. But the answer to bad jokes is not to ban all jokes. It is to encourage better jokes. We should be promoting comedy that challenges our assumptions, makes us think, and yes, even makes us uncomfortable.

But in this woke world, discomfort is seen as a cardinal sin. We must protect ourselves from any hint of discomfort or offense. We must shield ourselves from the harsh realities of life and live in a bubble of perpetual outrage. Well, I say enough is enough!

We need to reclaim the lost art of laughing at ourselves. We need to embrace comedy that pushes boundaries and challenges our preconceived notions. We need to be able to laugh at our own flaws and recognize that humor can be a powerful tool for growth and understanding.

So let us not be afraid to laugh, my dear reader. Let us not be afraid to find humor in the absurdities of life. Let us not be afraid to poke fun at ourselves and each other. For in laughter, we find common ground and the shared humanity that unites us all.

Finding Humor in a Woke World

Ah, the world of comedy. A place where laughter reigns supreme and no topic is off-limits. Or at least, it used to be. In this woke world we find ourselves in, comedy has become a minefield of potential offense and outrage. But fear not, dear reader, for even in this politically correct landscape, there are still ways to find humor and have a good laugh without offending anyone (well, almost anyone).

First and foremost, it's important to remember that laughter is a universal language. No matter who you are or where you come from, we all enjoy a good chuckle. So why not focus on the things that bring us together rather than tear us apart? Instead of making jokes about sensitive topics like race or gender, let's turn our attention to the absurdities of everyday life.

Take, for example, the trials and tribulations of modern technology. We've all been there - struggling to figure out how to use the latest gadget or dealing with the frustrations of an unreliable internet connection. These are the moments that unite us in our shared humanity and provide endless comedic material.

And let's not forget about the quirks and idiosyncrasies of human behavior. From awkward social interactions to bizarre habits, there's no shortage of material to mine for laughs. Just think about how many times you've found yourself in a situation that was so absurd, it could only be described as a comedy sketch waiting to happen.

Of course, it's important to approach comedy with a sense of empathy and understanding. While we may find humor in the foibles of others, it's crucial to remember that everyone has their own struggles and insecurities. Punching down or making fun of marginalized groups is never okay, but that doesn't mean we can't find humor in the universal experiences we all share.

In fact, some of the best comedy comes from shining a light on our own flaws and vulnerabilities. By embracing our imperfections and laughing at ourselves, we not only find humor but also foster a sense of humility and connection with others. After all, who hasn't had a moment of embarrassment or made a silly mistake?

So let's reclaim comedy from the clutches of political correctness and bring back the joy and laughter that it was meant to inspire. Let's focus on the absurdities of life and the shared experiences that unite us all. And most importantly, let's never forget the power of laughter to heal, connect, and remind us of our common humanity.

Chapter 5: Identity Politics and the Erosion of Individuality

Groupthink and Tribalism

Ah, groupthink and tribalism, the dynamic duo of identity politics. These two forces work together like peanut butter and jelly, or like politicians and empty promises. They are the driving forces behind the erosion of individuality and the rise of collective thinking.

You see, in the world of identity politics, it's not enough to just be an individual with your own thoughts and opinions. No, no, no. You must align yourself with a group, preferably one that shares your skin color, gender identity, or favorite flavor of ice cream.

And once you've found your tribe, you must adhere to their beliefs and values without question. Dissent is not allowed in this brave new world. If you dare to have a different opinion or challenge the status quo, you will be cast out faster than a Kardashian marriage.

But why would anyone willingly give up their individuality for the sake of fitting into a group? Well, my dear reader, it's all about that sweet sense of belonging. Humans are social creatures by nature, and we crave acceptance from our peers. So when we find a group that accepts us for who we are (or at least who we claim to be), it's hard to resist the allure.

But here's the thing about groupthink and tribalism: they're not exactly known for their critical thinking skills. When you're surrounded by people who all think the same way, it's easy to fall into a pattern of unquestioning conformity. You stop questioning your own beliefs and start parroting the party line.

And let me tell you, my friend, there is nothing more dangerous than a group of people who all think the same way. They become an echo chamber of their own ideas, reinforcing their own biases and shutting out any dissenting voices. It's like a cult, but with less Kool-Aid and more hashtags.

But don't worry, it's not all doom and gloom. There is hope for those who dare to be individuals in a world of groupthink. It starts with questioning the status quo and challenging the prevailing narrative. It means being open to different perspectives and engaging in thoughtful debate.

So next time you find yourself tempted to join a tribe or jump on the bandwagon of a popular cause, take a moment to pause and reflect. Ask yourself if you're truly aligning with your own values or if you're just following the crowd. Remember, true individuality is a precious thing, and it should never be sacrificed on the altar of groupthink.

The Danger of Identity Labels

Ah, identity labels. Those delightful little boxes we can neatly place ourselves in, like a game of human Tetris. It's like being a character in a video game, except instead of collecting coins and power-ups, we collect labels and victim points. How exciting!

But let's take a step back and think about this for a moment. What purpose do these labels serve? Are they really helping us understand ourselves and each other better? Or are they just another way to divide us into smaller and smaller groups until we're all alone in our own little corner of the world?

Identity labels have become the currency of the woke world. They're like those fancy limited edition sneakers that everyone wants to get their hands on. The more labels you have, the more woke you are. It's like a status symbol for the socially conscious.

But here's the thing about identity labels: they're reductive. They reduce complex individuals to a single word or phrase that is supposed to sum up their entire existence. It's like trying to capture the essence of a symphony in a single note. It just doesn't work.

Take me, for example. I'm a white, heterosexual, cisgender male. According to the woke handbook, that means I'm the epitome of privilege and oppression. But does that label really capture who I am as a person? Does it tell you anything about my hopes, dreams, fears, or aspirations? No, it doesn't.

Identity labels also create a dangerous us-versus-them mentality. They encourage tribalism and division, pitting one group against another in a never-ending battle for victimhood supremacy. It's like a never-ending game of who's more oppressed?

And let's not forget the pressure that comes with these labels. Once you've been assigned a label, you're expected to conform to certain expectations and beliefs. Step out of line and you risk being labeled a traitor to your own identity group.

But here's the thing: we are more than just our labels. We are complex individuals with unique experiences and perspectives. We shouldn't be defined by a single word or phrase.

So let's break free from the shackles of identity labels and embrace our individuality. Let's celebrate the things that make us different and find common ground with those who are different from us.

Because at the end of the day, we're all just human beings trying to navigate this crazy world together. And that's something worth celebrating.

Victimhood as Currency

Ah, victimhood. The holy grail of the woke movement. In this section, we will explore how victimhood has become a currency in the world of identity politics. It's like a twisted version of Monopoly, where instead of collecting properties, you collect oppression points.

In the woke world, being a victim is not just a state of being, it's a status symbol. The more oppressed you are, the higher your social standing. It's like a bizarre popularity contest where the winner is the one who has suffered the most.

But how does one become a victim? Well, it's

quite simple really. All you have to do is find some aspect of your identity that can be construed as marginalized or oppressed. It could be your race, gender, sexual orientation, or even your choice of breakfast cereal. Anything goes in the game of victimhood.

Once you've identified your victim status, it's time to cash in those oppression points. You can use them to gain sympathy, attention, and even special privileges. Need an extra day to finish that assignment? Just play the victim card and watch as your professor bends over backward to accommodate you.

But be careful not to overplay your hand. The woke community has a keen sense for detecting frauds and imposters. They can smell privilege from a mile away. So, if you're a straight white male claiming to be oppressed, you better have some solid evidence to back it up. Maybe a scar from a childhood game of tag gone wrong or a traumatic incident involving gluten.

Of course, there are some who argue that this obsession with victimhood is unhealthy and counterproductive. They say that it encourages people to focus on their grievances rather than their strengths. They believe that true empowerment comes from taking control of your own life, not from playing the victim.

But who needs empowerment when you can have pity? Who needs self-improvement when you can have special treatment? Who needs personal responsibility when you can blame society for all your problems?

In the woke world, victimhood is the ultimate trump card. It's like having a get-out-of-jail-free card in Monopoly. Except instead of getting out of jail, you get to silence anyone who disagrees with you. It's a powerful weapon, and it's being wielded with reckless abandon.

So, my dear reader, I leave you with this question: Are we really creating a more inclusive and equal society by turning victimhood into a currency? Or are we just perpetuating a culture of entitlement and division? The choice is yours.

Breaking Free from Identity

Shackles

Ah, identity politics. The never-ending quest to put people into neat little boxes and slap labels on them. It's like a game of human Tetris, but instead of trying to clear lines, we're trying to clear up any semblance of individuality. How fun!

But fear not, my friends! There is hope. We can break free from these identity shackles and reclaim our individuality. It won't be easy, but nothing worth doing ever is.

Step one: stop caring about what other people think. Seriously, it's exhausting trying to please everyone all the time. Just be yourself and let the chips fall where they may. If someone doesn't like you because of your race, gender, or whatever other label they want to slap on you, that's their problem, not yours.

Step two: embrace your contradictions. We're all walking contradictions, my friends. We're complex beings with a multitude of thoughts and feelings. So don't be afraid to have opinions that don't neatly fit into one ideological box or another. Embrace the messiness of being human.

Step three: challenge the status quo. Just because society tells you that you have to think or act a certain way based on your identity doesn't mean you have to listen. Break free from those expectations and forge your own path. Be a rebel with a cause, or without one. It's up to you.

Step four: surround yourself with diverse voices. Don't limit yourself to an echo chamber of people who think exactly like you do. Seek out different perspectives and engage in thoughtful conversations. You might just learn something new and expand your horizons.

Step five: celebrate your uniqueness. We're all special snowflakes, my friends. And I mean that in the best possible way. Embrace what makes you different and don't be afraid to let your freak flag fly. Life is too short to try and fit into someone else's mold.

And finally, step six: laugh at the absurdity of it all. Identity politics can be pretty ridiculous when you think about it. So why not find the humor in it? Laugh at the absurdity of trying to put seven billion people into neat little boxes. Laugh at the hypocrisy of those who claim to fight for equality while simultaneously dividing us into tribes. And most importantly, laugh at yourself. Life is too short to take everything so seriously.

So there you have it, my friends. A guide to breaking free from the shackles of identity politics and reclaiming your individuality. It won't be easy, but it will be worth it. Now go forth and be unapologetically yourself!

Celebrating Our Unique Identities

Ah, identity politics. The great divider. The champion of diversity and inclusivity that somehow manages to make everyone feel like they're walking on eggshells. But fear not, dear reader, for in this section we shall explore the wonderful world of celebrating our unique identities in a way that doesn't involve shouting at each other on Twitter.

You see, in the woke world, identity is everything. It's like a giant game of Guess Who? where instead of asking questions about physical features, you ask about someone's preferred pronouns and whether they've been properly educated on the latest intersectional theories. It's a minefield out there, folks.

But let's take a step back and remember that identity is not just about labels and categories. It's about the unique combination of experiences, beliefs, and quirks that make each of us who we are. And yes, that includes the fact that some of us still enjoy watching Friends reruns without feeling the need to write a 10-page thesis on its problematic themes.

So how do we celebrate our unique identities without getting caught up in the never-ending cycle of outrage? Well, for starters, we can embrace the idea that it's okay to have different opinions. Shocking, I know. But diversity of thought is just as important as diversity of race, gender, and all the other things we like to put in neat little boxes.

Instead of trying to silence those who disagree

with us, let's engage in respectful dialogue and actually listen to what they have to say. Who knows, we might even learn something. And if not, at least we'll have a good laugh when they inevitably say something ridiculous.

Another way to celebrate our unique identities is by embracing our hobbies and interests, no matter how unwoke they may be. If you want to spend your weekends binge-watching reality TV shows or collecting vintage action figures, go for it! Life is too short to worry about whether your guilty pleasures align with the latest social justice trends.

And let's not forget the importance of humor in celebrating our unique identities. Laughter is a universal language that can bring people together, even in the most politically correct of times. So go ahead and make that joke, as long as it's not at the expense of someone's humanity. We could all use a good laugh.

In conclusion, dear reader, let us celebrate our unique identities by embracing diversity of thought, indulging in our guilty pleasures, and finding humor in the absurdities of life. Let us remember that identity is not just about labels and categories, but about the rich tapestry of experiences that make each of us who we are.

And most importantly, let us never forget that we are all human beings, flawed and imperfect, but capable of growth and understanding. So let's put down our pitchforks, step away from the keyboard, and start celebrating the beautiful mess that is the human experience.

Chapter 6: Education in the Age of Wokeness

Indoctrination or Education?

Ah, education. The noble pursuit of knowledge, critical thinking, and preparing young minds for the challenges of the world. Or at least, that's what it used to be. In the age of wokeness, education has taken a detour down a treacherous path.

Gone are the days of teaching students how to think. Now, it's all about telling them what to think. And what they should think is that everything is racist, sexist, and oppressive. Hooray!

Instead of fostering intellectual curiosity and encouraging students to question everything, schools have become indoctrination centers for the woke agenda. It's like a never-ending episode of The Twilight Zone, where reality is turned upside down and common sense is thrown out the window.

Take history, for example. In the good old days, history was taught as a series of events and facts that shaped our world. But now, it's all about teaching students that everything they know is a lie and that America is irredeemably evil.

Forget about learning about the Founding Fathers and their noble ideals. Instead, let's focus on their flaws and paint them as nothing more than slave-owning racists. Because apparently, we can't have heroes anymore.

And don't even get me started on literature. The classics? Dead white men who have nothing to offer us in this enlightened age. Instead, let's read books written by people who check all the right boxes on the identity politics checklist.

But it's not just the content of education that has been hijacked by the woke brigade. It's also the way it's taught. Critical thinking? That's so last century. Now, it's all about critical theory.

Critical theory, for those lucky enough to be

blissfully unaware, is a fancy term for looking at everything through the lens of power dynamics and oppression. It's like putting on a pair of glasses that only allow you to see the world in shades of victimhood.

So instead of teaching students how to think for themselves, schools are teaching them how to be professional victims. They're being taught that their worth is determined by their identity and that they should view everything through the prism of oppression.

But hey, who needs critical thinking when you can have critical theory? Who needs facts when you can have feelings? Who needs logic when you can have identity politics?

So, is education in the age of wokeness really education? Or is it just indoctrination disguised as education? I'll let you be the judge.

The Bias in Textbooks and Curriculum

Ah, education. The noble pursuit of knowledge, the shaping of young minds, and the indoctrination of future generations. Wait, what was that last part? Yes, my dear reader, education has become a battleground for the woke warriors to impose their agenda upon unsuspecting students.

Let's start with textbooks. These hefty tomes are supposed to provide a balanced view of history and the world. But alas, they have fallen victim to the woke brigade. Gone are the days of objective facts and critical analysis. Now we have textbooks that read like propaganda pamphlets.

Take history textbooks, for example. They used to be filled with dates, events, and important figures. But now they're more interested in pushing a narrative than teaching actual history. Christopher Columbus? Oh no, he's not a brave explorer who discovered America. He's a genocidal maniac who single-handedly destroyed indigenous cultures.

And don't even get me started on literature textbooks. Shakespeare? Dead white guy who wrote some plays. Let's replace him with some obscure poet from a marginalized community that no one has ever heard of. Because diversity is more important than literary merit, right?

But it's not just the content of textbooks that's problematic. It's also the curriculum itself. The woke warriors have infiltrated every subject, from math to science to gym class. No subject is safe from their clutches.

In math class, they're teaching students about mathematical justice and how numbers are inherently racist. Apparently, 2+2 doesn't equal 4 anymore. It equals whatever you want it to be, as long as it aligns with your personal identity.

In science class, they're more interested in teaching students about gender theory than actual scientific principles. Forget about learning about atoms and molecules. Let's talk about how gender is a social construct and how we can deconstruct the patriarchy using test tubes and Bunsen burners.

And let's not forget gym class. It used to be a time for kids to run around and play sports. Now it's a time for kids to learn about body positivity and fat acceptance. Forget about winning or losing. Everyone gets a participation trophy because we don't want to hurt anyone's feelings.

The woke warriors have turned education into a minefield of political correctness and ideological indoctrination. They're more interested in pushing their agenda than actually teaching students critical thinking skills and preparing them for the real world.

So what can we do? Well, we can start by demanding that textbooks and curriculum be based on facts and evidence, not ideology. We can push back against the woke warriors and their attempts to rewrite history and science. And most importantly, we can teach our children to think for themselves and question everything they're taught.

Education should be about expanding minds, not narrowing them. It should be about fostering curiosity and intellectual growth, not pushing a political agenda. It's time to take back our schools from the woke warriors and return education to its rightful place as a beacon of knowledge and enlightenment.

Teaching Critical Thinking or Critical Theory?

Ah, critical thinking. The holy grail of education. The ability to analyze, evaluate, and question information. It's a skill that should be cherished and nurtured in our young minds. But alas, in the age of wokeness, critical thinking seems to have taken a backseat to critical theory.

Critical theory, for those not in the know, is a fancy term for a bunch of academic jargon that basically says everything is about power and oppression. It's like a conspiracy theory on steroids. According to critical theorists, every aspect of society is riddled with hidden power dynamics and systemic oppression. And if you dare to question this narrative, well, you're just another cog in the oppressive machine.

So instead of teaching our children how to think critically and independently, we're teaching them how to regurgitate the latest buzzwords and catchphrases. We're telling them that their worth as individuals is determined by their identity group and their ability to spout off the right talking points.

Gone are the days of open-minded debate and intellectual curiosity. Now it's all about who can virtue signal the loudest and who can claim the most victimhood points. It's like a twisted game show where the winner gets a pat on the back and a lifetime supply of self-righteousness.

But what about teaching our children how to think for themselves? What about encouraging them to question authority and challenge prevailing narratives? Oh no, that's too dangerous. We can't have our little snowflakes thinking for themselves. They might come to the wrong conclusions and offend someone's delicate sensibilities.

And so, critical theory reigns supreme in our classrooms. We're told that it's the only way to dismantle oppressive systems and create a more just society. But here's the thing: critical theory is not the same as critical thinking. It's a one-size-fits-all ideology that leaves no room for dissent or nuance.

In the name of social justice, we're sacrificing intellectual diversity and stifling free thought. We're creating a generation of ideological robots who can recite the party line but can't think for themselves. And that's not education, my friends. That's indoctrination.

So let's bring back critical thinking. Let's teach our children how to question, how to analyze, and how to form their own opinions. Let's encourage them to explore different perspectives and challenge prevailing wisdom. Let's give them the tools they need to navigate this complex world with an open mind and a healthy dose of skepticism.

Because at the end of the day, education should be about expanding minds, not narrowing them. It should be about fostering intellectual curiosity, not promoting ideological conformity. And it should be about teaching our children how to think, not what to think.

So let's reclaim critical thinking from the clutches

of critical theory. Let's empower our children to question authority and challenge prevailing narratives. Let's create a generation of independent thinkers who are unafraid to speak their minds and stand up for what they believe in.

Because in the end, it's not about being woke or unwoke. It's about being awake. Awake to the world around us, awake to different perspectives, and awake to the power of our own minds.

Navigating the Minefield of Campus Activism

Ah, campus activism. The hallowed ground where young minds go to be molded into woke warriors. It's like a boot camp for social justice, where students learn to march in lockstep with the latest progressive fads and fancies. But navigating this minefield of activism can be quite the challenge.

First, you have to choose your cause. Will it be

climate change? Gender equality? Racial justice? Or maybe you want to go all out and fight for the rights of endangered unicorns. The possibilities are endless!

Once you've picked your cause, it's time to join a student group. There's the Save the Whales club, the Ban Plastic Straws society, and of course, the ever-popular Vegan Liberation Front. Just make sure you don't accidentally join the Meat Eaters Anonymous club. That could get awkward.

Now that you're part of a group, it's time to plan your protests. Remember, the key to a successful protest is catchy slogans and eye-catching signs. Save the Planet, Save Your Soul! Equal Rights for Unicorns! Down with Patriarchy, Up with Puppies! Get creative, people!

But be careful not to offend anyone. You wouldn't want to accidentally appropriate someone else's cause or step on any toes. It's a delicate dance, this activism thing. One wrong move and you could find yourself canceled faster than you can say microaggression.

And speaking of microaggressions, be prepared for some serious call-out culture. If you accidentally use the wrong pronoun or forget to check your privilege at the door, you'll be called out faster than you can say I'm sorry, I didn't mean to offend. It's like walking on eggshells, but instead of eggs, it's fragile egos.

Of course, no campus activism experience would be complete without a good old-fashioned protest. Grab your megaphone and your picket signs and hit the streets! Just make sure you have a permit and stay within the designated protest zone. We wouldn't want any accidental jaywalking now, would we?

But remember, activism isn't just about shouting slogans and waving signs. It's also about creating safe spaces where everyone feels comfortable expressing their opinions. So if someone disagrees with you, just remember to listen and validate their feelings... as long as their feelings align with yours, of course.

And finally, don't forget to document every moment of your activism journey on social media. Because if it's not on Instagram, did it really happen? Plus, you'll need all those likes and retweets to prove just how woke you are.

So there you have it, the minefield of campus activism. It's a wild ride, full of passion, righteousness, and the occasional vegan potluck. Just remember to stay woke, stay safe, and most importantly, stay away from those meat-eating support groups. Trust me, they're a recipe for disaster.

The Importance of Intellectual Diversity

Ah, intellectual diversity. Two words that seem to have gone extinct in the age of wokeness. In the hallowed halls of academia, where once ideas clashed and minds were expanded, now there is only one acceptable way of thinking. And if you dare to deviate from the woke orthodoxy, well, you can kiss your reputation and career goodbye.

Gone are the days when universities were a marketplace of ideas. Now they are more like a monopoly board where only one ideology reigns supreme. It's like playing a game of Monopoly with only one player - it's not much fun and it's certainly not fair.

But why is intellectual diversity so important? Well, let me tell you a little story. Once upon a time, there was a group of people who thought the Earth was flat. They were so convinced of their belief that they refused to listen to anyone who disagreed with them. They silenced dissenting voices and persecuted those who dared to challenge their worldview.

Now, imagine if there had been intellectual diversity back then. Imagine if there had been people who questioned the prevailing wisdom and offered alternative theories. Maybe we would have discovered that the Earth is actually round a lot sooner.

Intellectual diversity is like a safety net for society. It ensures that no one ideology becomes too powerful or too dominant. It allows for the free exchange of ideas and encourages critical thinking. It challenges us to question our own beliefs and consider alternative perspectives.

But in the age of wokeness, intellectual diversity is seen as a threat. It's seen as a dangerous idea that must be silenced and suppressed. The woke elite want everyone to think the same way they do, and they will stop at nothing to achieve their goal.

They claim to be champions of diversity and inclusion, but when it comes to intellectual diversity, they are nowhere to be found. They preach tolerance and acceptance, but only if you agree with them. If you dare to have a different opinion, well, you can expect to be canceled faster than you can say thoughtcrime.

But here's the thing - intellectual diversity is not just important for the sake of fairness or open-mindedness. It's important because it leads to better ideas and better solutions. When people with different perspectives come together and engage in respectful debate, amazing things can happen.

Innovation thrives on intellectual diversity. Progress depends on it. Without it, we are doomed to stagnation and conformity.

So let's not allow the woke elite to dictate what we can and cannot think. Let's reclaim intellectual diversity and bring it back into our universities, our workplaces, and our society. Let's celebrate the power of different ideas and the beauty of respectful debate.

Because in the end, it's not about being right or wrong. It's about being open to new possibilities and embracing the richness that comes from intellectual diversity.

So let's raise a toast to intellectual diversity - may it never be silenced or suppressed again!

Chapter 7: The Woke Economy

Corporate Virtue Signaling

Ah, the woke economy. A place where corporations compete not only for profits, but also for the title of Most Virtuous Company. It's a race to see who can signal their virtue the loudest and the proudest. And let me tell you, it's quite the spectacle.

Gone are the days when companies focused solely on providing a quality product or service. Now, they must also prove their commitment to social justice causes. It's not enough to make a good widget; you must also be seen as a champion of diversity, inclusion, and all things woke.

But here's the thing: most of this corporate virtue signaling is nothing more than empty gestures and PR stunts. It's all about appearances, my friends. Take, for example, the trend of companies changing their logos to incorporate rainbow colors during Pride Month.

It's a nice gesture, sure, but what does it really accomplish? Does it actually help LGBTQ+ individuals in any meaningful way? Or is it just a way for companies to pat themselves on the back and say, Look at us! We're so inclusive!

And let's not forget about those cringe-worthy commercials that try to tackle social issues in 30 seconds or less. You know the ones I'm talking about. They feature a diverse cast of characters holding hands and singing Kumbaya while a voiceover tells us how this company is making the world a better place. It's like they're trying to sell us laundry detergent and social justice at the same time.

But perhaps the most egregious form of corporate virtue signaling is when companies jump on the bandwagon of the latest social justice trend without actually doing anything to address the underlying issues. They'll release a statement condemning racism or sexism or whatever is currently in vogue, but behind closed doors, they continue to engage in discriminatory practices. It's all about optics, my friends. As long as they look good on the surface, they can continue with business as usual.

Now, don't get me wrong. I'm not saying that companies shouldn't strive to be socially responsible. In fact, I believe that businesses have a role to play in addressing societal issues. But let's not confuse virtue signaling with real action. It's easy to change your logo or release a statement; it's much harder to actually make meaningful changes within your organization.

So, the next time you see a company proclaiming their commitment to social justice, take a moment to dig a little deeper. Are they actually walking the walk, or are they just talking the talk? Because in the woke economy, appearances can be deceiving. And sometimes, the loudest virtue signalers are the ones with the most skeletons in their closets.

Diversity and Inclusion - A Double-Edged Sword

Ah, diversity and inclusion. The buzzwords of the woke economy. Companies everywhere are falling over themselves to prove just how diverse and inclusive they are. It's like a competition to see who can virtue signal the loudest.

But let's take a step back and examine this whole diversity and inclusion thing. On the surface, it sounds great. Who wouldn't want a workplace that celebrates different backgrounds and perspectives? But like most things in the world of wokeness, it's not as simple as it seems.

First of all, let's talk about diversity. Companies are obsessed with having a diverse workforce. They want people of different races, genders, sexual orientations, and whatever other boxes they can tick. But here's the thing: diversity should be about more than just ticking boxes.

True diversity is about diversity of thought. It's about having people with different ideas and perspectives coming together to solve problems and drive innovation. But in the woke economy, diversity often means hiring based on quotas rather than qualifications.

So you end up with a workplace full of people who may look different on the outside but think exactly the same on the inside. It's like a diversity Potemkin village, where everything looks diverse and inclusive from the outside, but it's all just a facade.

And then there's inclusion. Companies love to talk about how inclusive they are. They have diversity training programs and employee resource groups and all sorts of initiatives to make everyone feel included. But again, it's not always what it seems.

Inclusion should be about creating an environment where everyone feels valued and respected, regardless of their background or identity. But in the woke economy, inclusion often means silencing anyone who doesn't toe the party line.

If you dare to have a different opinion or question the prevailing narrative, you're labeled as problematic or unwoke. Your ideas are dismissed and you're made to feel like an outsider in your own workplace. So much for inclusion.

But hey, at least the company can pat itself on

the back for being diverse and inclusive, right? Who cares if they're actually stifling free thought and creating an echo chamber?

The truth is, diversity and inclusion should be about more than just empty gestures and virtue signaling. They should be about creating a truly inclusive environment where everyone feels welcome and respected, regardless of their background or beliefs.

So let's stop with the quotas and the performative allyship. Let's focus on fostering real diversity of thought and creating workplaces where people can speak their minds without fear of retribution. Only then can we truly reap the benefits of a diverse and inclusive workforce.

The Myth of the Gender Pay Gap

Ah, the gender pay gap. It's like the Loch Ness Monster of the corporate world. Everyone's heard of it, but no one's actually seen it. It's a mythical creature that lurks in the depths of feminist literature and social justice campaigns. But is it real? Or is it just another figment of our collective imagination?

Let's take a closer look at this elusive beast. According to the narrative, women are paid less than men for doing the same job. It's a simple equation: man does work, man gets paid more; woman does work, woman gets paid less. But like most things in life, it's not that simple.

First of all, let's consider the fact that men and women tend to choose different careers. Men are more likely to go into fields like engineering and finance, which tend to pay more. Women, on the other hand, are more likely to choose careers in education and healthcare, which tend to pay less. It's not because society is forcing them into these roles; it's because they have different interests and priorities.

But even within the same field, there are differences in pay between men and women. However, these differences can often be explained by factors other than discrimination. For example, men are more likely to negotiate for higher salaries, while women tend to be more hesitant. It's not that employers are intentionally paying women less; it's that women are less likely to ask for more.

Another factor to consider is the issue of work-life balance. Women are more likely to take time off or work part-time to care for children or elderly parents. This can have an impact on their earning potential and career progression. It's not that employers are penalizing women for having families; it's that they're taking into account the fact that these women may not be able to commit as much time and energy to their jobs.

Now, I'm not saying that there aren't cases of discrimination in the workplace. There are certainly instances where women are paid less than men for doing the same job. But these cases are the exception, not the rule. The vast majority of the gender pay gap can be explained by factors other than discrimination.

So why does the myth of the gender pay gap persist? Well, it's a useful tool for those who want to push a certain agenda. It allows them to portray women as perpetual victims and men as oppressors. It creates a sense of outrage and injustice that can be harnessed for political gain.

But here's the thing: perpetuating this myth does a disservice to both men and women. It undermines the achievements of women who have succeeded in their chosen fields through hard work and determination. It also perpetuates the idea that men are inherently privileged and oppressive, which is simply not true.

So let's put an end to this myth once and for all. Let's stop blaming discrimination for every difference in outcome between men and women. Let's recognize that men and women are different, and that's okay. Let's focus on creating a society where everyone has equal opportunities to succeed, regardless of their gender.

And if you still believe in the gender pay gap, I have a bridge to sell you. It's located right next to the Loch Ness Monster's lair.

Affirmative Action or Reverse Discrimination?

Ah, affirmative action. The great equalizer. Or is it? In the world of identity politics, affirmative action has become a hotly debated topic. On one side, we have those who argue that it is a necessary tool to level the playing field and address historical injustices. On the other side, we have those who claim that it is nothing more than reverse discrimination.

Let's take a closer look at this issue, shall we? Affirmative action was originally intended to provide opportunities for marginalized groups who had been historically disadvantaged. The idea was to give them a leg up in areas such as education and employment. Sounds fair, right? Well, not so fast.

The problem with affirmative action is that it often ends up discriminating against individuals who are not part of the favored groups. Imagine you're a white male applying for a job or trying to get into college. You may find yourself at a disadvantage simply because of your race and gender. Is that fair? Is it fair to punish someone for something they have no control over?

But wait, you say, affirmative action is necessary

to address historical injustices! Well, let me ask you this: how far back do we go? Do we only consider the injustices of the past few centuries or do we go all the way back to the dawn of time? And what about individuals who have never experienced any form of discrimination? Should they be penalized simply because they happen to belong to a certain group?

The truth is, affirmative action has become a blunt instrument that often fails to achieve its intended goals. It may provide temporary relief for some individuals, but it does little to address the root causes of inequality. In fact, it often perpetuates stereotypes and reinforces divisions between different groups.

So what's the solution? Well, instead of focusing on identity, why not focus on merit? Let's create a society where individuals are judged based on their abilities and qualifications, rather than their race or gender. Let's provide equal opportunities for everyone, regardless of their background. Let's level the playing field by investing in education and creating a fair and transparent system.

Of course, this is easier said than done. It

requires a shift in mindset and a willingness to challenge the status quo. But if we truly want to create a society that is fair and just, we must be willing to have these difficult conversations and explore alternative solutions.

So the next time you hear someone advocating for affirmative action, ask yourself: is this really the best way to address inequality? Or are there better, more effective ways to achieve our goals? Let's move beyond identity politics and focus on what truly matters: creating a society where everyone has an equal opportunity to succeed.

Capitalism vs. Social Justice

Ah, capitalism. The great engine of innovation and prosperity. The system that has lifted millions out of poverty and created a world of abundance. But wait! Hold your horses! Here come the woke warriors to rain on capitalism's parade.

You see, according to the woke elite, capitalism is the root of all evil. It's the system that perpetuates inequality and oppresses the marginalized. It's the reason why some people have more than others. And we can't have that, can we?

So what's their solution? Social justice, of course! Because nothing says let's fix inequality like taking away people's hard-earned money and redistributing it to those who didn't earn it.

But here's the thing: capitalism isn't perfect. No system is. But it's the best we've got. It's the system that rewards hard work and innovation. It's the system that allows individuals to pursue their dreams and create a better life for themselves and their families.

And let's not forget about competition. You know, that thing that drives innovation and pushes companies to constantly improve? Well, according to the woke warriors, competition is just another form of oppression. It's the reason why some companies succeed and others fail. And we can't have that, can we?

So instead of embracing competition and allowing the market to determine winners and losers, the woke warriors want to level the playing field. They want to give everyone a participation trophy and ensure that no one feels left out.

But here's the problem with that approach: when everyone gets a trophy, no one gets a trophy. When you take away the incentives to work hard and succeed, you end up with a society where mediocrity is celebrated and excellence is punished.

And let's not forget about personal responsibility. You know, that thing that says you're in control of your own destiny? Well, according to the woke warriors, personal responsibility is just another form of victim-blaming. It's the reason why some people succeed and others fail. And we can't have that, can we?

So instead of encouraging individuals to take control of their own lives and make responsible choices, the woke warriors want to blame society for their problems. They want to play the victim card and demand that others fix their mistakes.

But here's the reality: personal responsibility is

empowering. It's what allows individuals to overcome adversity and achieve greatness. It's what separates those who succeed from those who fail.

So let's not throw capitalism out with the bathwater. Let's not abandon the system that has brought us so much prosperity and opportunity. Instead, let's work to make capitalism more inclusive and equitable. Let's address the flaws in the system without throwing the baby out with the bathwater.

Because here's the truth: capitalism and social justice are not mutually exclusive. We can have a system that rewards hard work and innovation while also ensuring that everyone has a fair shot at success.

So let's stop demonizing capitalism and start working towards a society where everyone has the opportunity to thrive. Let's embrace the power of free markets and individual liberty. And let's reject the false choice between capitalism and social justice.

Chapter 8: The Devastating Effects of Identity Politics on Children

The Sacrifice of Proper Education on The Altar of Identity Politics

Ah, children. Those innocent little beings who are supposed to spend their days learning about the world and discovering their passions. Well, not anymore! Thanks to the wonders of identity politics, we have managed to turn education into a minefield of political correctness and ideological indoctrination.

Gone are the days when children could simply learn math, science, and history. No, now they must also learn about their privilege or lack thereof, their gender identity or lack thereof, and every other aspect of their identity that can be neatly categorized and put into a box.

Forget about critical thinking and intellectual curiosity. We must prioritize teaching children about the latest buzzwords and social justice issues. Who needs to know how to read when you can recite the entire glossary of intersectionality?

And let's not forget about the textbooks. Oh boy, those textbooks are a real treat. They have been carefully curated to ensure that every historical figure is judged solely by today's standards. Forget about understanding the context of their time or appreciating the complexities of history. We must judge them harshly and erase them from our collective memory if they don't meet our woke criteria.

But hey, who needs a well-rounded education when you can have a one-sided ideological agenda shoved down your throat? Who needs to learn about different perspectives and ideas when you can just parrot the latest woke talking points?

And let's not forget about the teachers. Poor souls who used to dream of inspiring young minds and fostering a love of learning. Now they must navigate the treacherous waters of political correctness and walk on eggshells to avoid offending anyone.

God forbid a teacher accidentally misgenders a student or fails to acknowledge their preferred pronouns. That would be a crime against humanity! We must prioritize the feelings of individuals over the pursuit of knowledge and intellectual growth.

So, congratulations, identity politics. You have successfully sacrificed proper education on the altar of political correctness. Our children are now well-versed in virtue signaling and social justice jargon, but they couldn't tell you the capital of their own country if their lives depended on it.

But hey, at least they know how to identify as a non-binary vegan unicorn with an affinity for interpretive dance. Who needs knowledge when you have identity?

Let Kids be Kids – Please!

Ah, the joys of childhood. A time when kids should be free to explore, play, and eat dirt without a care in the world. But alas, in the age of identity politics, even the innocent act of being a child is not spared from the clutches of woke ideology.

You see, children are no longer allowed to simply be children. They must now identify themselves with a myriad of labels and categories. It's like they're playing a never-ending game of Guess Who? but instead of asking if their opponent has glasses or a mustache, they're asking if they identify as male or female, cisgender or transgender, gay or straight, and the list goes on.

Gone are the days when kids could just be kids. Now they have to worry about which box to check on a form or which pronouns to use. It's enough to make any child's head spin.

But why stop at just one label? Why not pile on as many as possible? After all, the more labels you have, the more woke points you earn. It's like collecting trading cards, but instead of Pokemon or baseball players, you're collecting identities.

And let's not forget the pressure that comes with choosing the right identity. Kids are constantly bombarded with messages telling them that they must fit into a certain mold or else they're not being true to themselves. It's like a never-ending game of Who Am I? where the stakes are your very identity.

But here's the thing: children are still figuring out who they are. They're still learning and growing and exploring the world around them. They shouldn't be forced to conform to some predetermined set of identities.

Instead of pressuring kids to identify, we should be encouraging them to embrace their individuality. Let them be whoever they want to be, whether that's a princess or a pirate, a scientist or an artist. Let them explore different interests and try on different identities like they're trying on clothes at a dress-up party.

And let's not forget that children are resilient. They have an incredible capacity for growth and change. So why limit them with labels? Why not let them evolve and discover themselves at their own pace?

In the end, it's not about fitting into a box or checking off a list of identities. It's about allowing children to be true to themselves, whatever that may look like. So let's take the pressure off and let kids just be kids.

The Scourge of The Crime Against Humanity That Is: Gender Reassignment of Minors

Ah, the wonders of modern medicine! We live in an age where we can change our gender as easily as we change our socks. Well, maybe not quite that easily, but you get the idea. Gender reassignment surgery has become all the rage, and it seems that everyone and their dog wants to jump on the bandwagon.

But hold on a minute! Are we really okay with allowing minors to make such life-altering decisions? I mean, come on! These are kids we're talking about here. They can't even decide what flavor of ice cream they want, let alone whether they want to permanently alter their bodies.

Now, I'm not saying that gender dysphoria isn't a real thing. It absolutely is, and it's a struggle that many people face. But let's not forget that children are still developing both physically and mentally. Their brains are like sponges, soaking up information and experiences at an alarming rate. So why on earth would we allow them to make irreversible decisions about their gender? It's like giving a toddler a chainsaw and telling them to go wild in the backyard. Sure, they might think it's fun at first, but they'll quickly realize that they've made a huge mistake. And by then, it's too late.

But the woke brigade doesn't seem to care about such trivial matters as long-term consequences. No, they're too busy patting themselves on the back for being so progressive and inclusive. They'll tell you that allowing minors to undergo gender reassignment surgery is a matter of affirming their identity and protecting their mental health. Well, forgive me for being skeptical, but I fail to see how permanently altering a child's body is in any way beneficial for their mental health.

And let's not forget about the doctors who are willing to perform these procedures. I mean, seriously? Are they really so desperate for business that they're willing to slice and dice children? It's like something out of a horror movie. Coming soon to a theater near you: Dr. Frankenstein and the Gender Reassignment Clinic!

But perhaps the most disturbing aspect of all this is the fact that parents are actually encouraging their children to undergo these procedures. I mean, what kind of parent would willingly subject their child to such a traumatic experience? It's like they're playing God, deciding who their child should be before they've even had a chance to figure it out for themselves.

So, my dear readers, let us not be swayed by the siren song of the woke brigade. Let us stand firm in our belief that children should be allowed to grow and develop at their own pace, free from the pressures of gender reassignment surgery.

Let us protect our children from the butchery of gender reassignment and instead focus on providing them with love, support, and guidance as they navigate the complexities of their own identities.

And if anyone tries to tell you otherwise, just remember: common sense is a superpower in a world gone mad. Use it wisely.

Protecting Our Children from The Butchery of 'Gender Reassignment'

Ah, the wonders of modern medicine! We live in an age where we can change our gender as easily as we change our socks. It's like a buffet of identities, where you can pick and choose whatever you fancy. But what about the children? Are they also invited to this gender-swapping extravaganza?

Well, it seems that some people believe so. They argue that children should have the right to decide their gender at a young age. Forget about playing with toys or climbing trees; let's focus on choosing our gender instead! It's like a twisted version of Pin the Tail on the Donkey, except instead of a tail, it's your genitals.

Now, I'm all for freedom and self-expression, but let's not forget that children are still developing both physically and mentally. They're like little sponges, absorbing everything around them. So why are we encouraging them to make life-altering decisions before they even hit puberty?

The argument goes something like this: If a child identifies as a different gender, we should support them and help them transition. But hold on a minute! Isn't it our job as adults to guide and protect children? Shouldn't we be teaching them about the world and helping them navigate through life, rather than indulging their every whim?

Let's not forget that gender reassignment is a serious medical procedure. It involves hormone therapy, surgery, and a lifetime of medical interventions. It's not something to be taken lightly, like choosing a new hairstyle or getting a tattoo.

But the proponents of early gender transition argue that it's necessary to prevent mental health issues and suicide among transgender children. And while it's true that transgender individuals face higher rates of mental health problems, is gender reassignment really the solution?

There's a growing body of research that suggests otherwise. A study published in the Journal of the American Academy of Child and Adolescent Psychiatry found that the majority of children who experience gender dysphoria will eventually grow out of it and identify with their biological sex.

So why are we rushing to perform irreversible surgeries on children who may simply be going through a phase? It's like giving a toddler a tattoo because they said they wanted one. Sure, they might think it's cool now, but what about when they're older?

We need to protect our children from the butchery of 'gender reassignment.' Let them be kids and explore their interests without pushing adult concepts onto them. Let them grow and develop naturally, without subjecting them to unnecessary medical interventions.

And if they do eventually decide to transition, let's make sure they're old enough to fully understand the consequences and make an informed decision. Let's not rush them into something they may regret later on.

So, parents, teachers, and society as a whole, let's protect our children from the dangers of early gender reassignment. Let's give them the time and space to figure out who they are without subjecting them to unnecessary medical procedures. After all, childhood is a precious time that should be filled with laughter, play, and discovery, not surgeries and hormone therapy.

The Pressure on Children to Identify

Ah, childhood. A time of innocence, wonder, and relentless pressure to identify as something other than a child. Yes, my friends, in the wacky world of identity politics, even children are not spared from the clutches of labeling and categorization.

Gone are the days when kids could simply be kids. Now they must navigate the treacherous waters of identity and choose a label that will define them for the rest of their lives. It's like asking a toddler to pick their favorite Shakespeare play or a kindergartener to decide on their preferred investment strategy. It's absurd!

But fear not, dear reader, for I am here to guide you through this nonsensical maze of identity pressure. Let us begin with the most basic question: What do you identify as?

Now, if you're thinking that this question is reserved for adults who have had years of self-discovery and introspection under their belts, think again. Children as young as three or four are being asked to identify their gender, their sexual orientation, and even their political beliefs.

Picture this scene: a group of preschoolers sitting in a circle, their tiny legs crossed, as their teacher asks each of them to share their preferred pronouns. I identify as a unicorn, says little Timmy, while Sally proudly declares, I identify as a dinosaur. And let's not forget about little Jimmy, who confidently proclaims, I identify as a superhero who fights against the tyranny of nap time.

Now, call me old-fashioned, but shouldn't children be allowed to just be children? Shouldn't they be free to explore the world around them without the burden of having to fit into a predetermined box?

But no, in the twisted world of identity politics, children must conform to the latest trends and ideologies. They must choose a label and wear it like a badge of honor. And woe betide those who dare to question or deviate from the norm.

Imagine little Johnny, a curious and imaginative child who loves playing with dolls and trucks alike. One day, he decides to wear a dress because it makes him feel happy and free. But instead of celebrating his individuality and creativity, society tells him that he must be transgender or non-binary.

And so begins Johnny's journey down the rabbit hole of identity politics. He is bombarded with questions about his gender identity and forced to attend therapy sessions where he is told that his love for dolls is a sign of his true gender.

But what if Johnny just likes playing with dolls? What if he doesn't want to be labeled or categorized? What if he just wants to be a kid?

It's time we put an end to this madness and allow children to be children. Let them explore, let them play, and let them discover who they are at their own pace. Let's stop pressuring them to identify as something other than what they truly are: innocent, curious, and full of boundless potential.

So the next time you encounter a child, resist the urge to ask them about their gender identity or political beliefs. Instead, ask them about their favorite toy or what they want to be when they grow up. Let's give our children the gift of childhood and protect them from the suffocating pressure of identity politics.

The Fallacy of Non-Binary Children

Ah, non-binary children. The latest trend in the ever-expanding buffet of gender identities. It seems like every day there's a new gender popping up like a whack-a-mole at a carnival. And now we have non-binary children. How delightful!

Now, I don't want to sound like an old fogey who's stuck in the past, but when I was a child, we had two genders: boys and girls. Simple as that. You were either one or the other. None of this non-binary nonsense.

But apparently, we've evolved since then. Now we have children who identify as neither boys nor girls. They're some magical combination of both or neither or who knows what. It's like trying to solve a Rubik's Cube blindfolded while riding a unicycle.

Now, don't get me wrong. I'm all for people expressing themselves and finding their true identities. But when it comes to children, shouldn't we let them be kids first? I mean, they're still figuring out how to tie their shoelaces and use a fork properly. Do we really expect them to understand the complexities of gender identity?

And let's not forget the role of parents in all of this. It used to be that parents would guide their children through life, teaching them right from wrong, helping them navigate the treacherous waters of adolescence. But now, it seems like parents are just following their children's lead, trying to keep up with their ever-changing identities.

Imagine this scenario: little Timmy comes home from school one day and says, Mom, Dad, I'm non-binary. And instead of responding with a confused look and a What on earth does that mean?, the parents just nod and say, Oh, that's nice dear. Would you like some mac and cheese for dinner?

It's like we've entered an alternate reality where children are the ones in charge. They dictate the rules and we all have to follow along like obedient little sheep. Well, I don't know about you, but I'm not ready to hand over the reins to a bunch of kids who can't even decide what flavor ice cream they want.

So let's take a step back and think about what we're doing here. Are we really helping these children by encouraging them to identify as non-binary? Or are we just adding another layer of confusion to their already chaotic lives?

Maybe instead of obsessing over labels and identities, we should focus on teaching our children the values that truly matter: kindness, empathy, and respect for others. Because at the end of the day, it doesn't matter if you're a boy, a girl, or a non-binary unicorn. What matters is how you treat the people around you.

So let's put an end to this non-binary madness and let children be children. Let them play, explore, and discover who they are without the pressure of conforming to some arbitrary gender identity. Because in the grand scheme of things, it really doesn't matter if you're a boy, a girl, or something in between. What matters is that you're happy and true to yourself.

The Impact of Identity Politics on Mental Health in Children

Ah, the delicate minds of children. So pure, so innocent, and yet so vulnerable to the pernicious influence of identity politics. It's truly a tragedy. You see, dear reader, when we subject our children to the toxic ideology of identity politics, we are not only robbing them of their individuality but also putting their mental health at risk.

Imagine a world where children are constantly bombarded with messages that tell them they must fit into predefined boxes based on their race, gender, or sexual orientation. It's like being trapped in a never-ending game of Guess Who? where your worth is determined solely by the color of your skin or the genitals you possess. Is this really the kind of world we want for our children?

The impact of identity politics on children's mental health cannot be overstated. It creates a breeding ground for anxiety and depression as children grapple with the pressure to conform to societal expectations. They are constantly questioning their own identities and feeling inadequate if they don't fit neatly into one of the predetermined categories.

But it doesn't stop there. Identity politics also fosters a culture of victimhood among children. They are taught to see themselves as oppressed or oppressors based on their identity, perpetuating a cycle of resentment and division. Instead of encouraging resilience and self-confidence, we are raising a generation of fragile individuals who believe they are entitled to special treatment because of their identity.

And let's not forget the impact of social media on children's mental health. In this digital age, children are constantly bombarded with images and messages that reinforce the narrow confines of identity politics. They compare themselves to carefully curated online personas and feel inadequate if they don't measure up. It's a never-ending cycle of self-doubt and insecurity.

So, what can we do to protect our children from the damaging effects of identity politics on their mental health? First and foremost, we must teach them the value of individuality and self-acceptance. We need to instill in them the belief that their worth is not determined by their identity but by their character and actions.

We also need to create spaces where children can explore their interests and passions without the pressure to conform to societal expectations. Let them be free to discover who they truly are without being confined by labels or stereotypes.

And finally, we must encourage open dialogue and critical thinking. Teach our children to question the narratives they are presented with and think for themselves. Help them understand that diversity of thought is just as important as diversity of identity.

In conclusion, dear reader, let us not sacrifice the mental health of our children on the altar of identity politics. Let us instead foster an environment of individuality, self-acceptance, and critical thinking. Only then can we truly protect our children from the harmful effects of this divisive ideology.

The Role of Parents in Navigating Identity Politics for Their Children

Ah, parents. Those poor souls who thought their biggest challenge would be getting their kids to eat their vegetables or do their homework. Little did they know that they would also have to navigate the treacherous waters of identity politics. It's like trying to sail a dinghy through a hurricane while juggling flaming swords. Fun times!

So, dear parents, how can you ensure that your child doesn't get swept away by the tsunami of identity politics? Well, fear not! I have some handy tips for you:

Tip #1: Teach them that they are more than

just their identity

Identity politics wants to reduce us all to a single label. But we are so much more than that! Teach your child that they are not defined solely by their race, gender, or any other identity marker. They are complex individuals with unique talents, interests, and quirks. And if they can juggle flaming swords while sailing a dinghy through a hurricane, well, that's just an added bonus.

Tip #2: Encourage critical thinking

Identity politics thrives on unquestioning adherence to a particular ideology. But critical thinking is its kryptonite. Teach your child to question everything, including the prevailing narratives of identity politics. Help them develop the skills to analyze arguments, evaluate evidence, and form their own opinions. Who knows, they might even become the next Socrates or Plato. Or at least win a few debates at the dinner table.

Tip #3: Expose them to diverse

perspectives

Identity politics loves echo chambers. But diversity of thought is like a cold shower for its warm and fuzzy feelings. Expose your child to a wide range of perspectives and encourage them to engage in respectful dialogue with people who hold different views. This will not only broaden their horizons but also help them develop empathy and understanding. Plus, it'll make family gatherings way more interesting.

Tip #4: Teach them resilience

Identity politics can be a tough nut to crack. It's like trying to argue with a brick wall that's armed with a megaphone. But resilience is key. Teach your child that they will encounter challenges and opposition along their journey, but they should never let it deter them from being true to themselves. And if all else fails, remind them that you have an unlimited supply of ice cream in the freezer.

Tip #5: Lead by example

Children are like sponges. They absorb everything around them, including your attitudes and behaviors. So, if you want to raise a child who can navigate the murky waters of identity politics with grace and humor, you need to lead by example. Show them what it means to be open-minded, respectful, and independent-minded. And don't forget to throw in a few dad jokes along the way.

So there you have it, dear parents. Your survival guide to navigating identity politics for your children. Remember, it's a wild ride out there, but with a little humor and a lot of love, you can help your child stay true to themselves in this crazy world.

The Influence of Social Media on Children's Identity Development

Ah, social media. The modern-day oracle where children seek validation, acceptance, and the perfect filter for their selfies. It's a magical place where kids can curate their online personas and pretend to be someone they're not. Truly, a paradise for identity politics.

Thanks to social media, children can now explore a myriad of identities without ever leaving their bedrooms. They can be a gender-fluid unicorn one day and a pansexual mermaid the next. It's like playing dress-up, but with hashtags and emojis.

But let's not forget the real heroes in this story: the parents. Yes, parents play a crucial role in navigating their children through the treacherous waters of social media identity development. It's like being a tour guide in a theme park filled with filters and influencers.

First and foremost, parents must ensure that their children have access to the latest smartphones and unlimited data plans. How else will they keep up with the ever-changing trends and hashtags? It's like giving them the keys to their own identity kingdom.

Next, parents should encourage their children to follow as many woke influencers as possible. These influencers are like modern-day philosophers, guiding our children towards enlightenment through carefully curated posts about self-love and body positivity.

Of course, parents must also monitor their children's online activities to protect them from any harmful content or ideas that might challenge their carefully constructed identities. We wouldn't want them questioning their beliefs or exploring different perspectives now, would we?

Parents should also encourage their children to engage in online activism. After all, what better way to solidify their identities than by joining virtual mobs and canceling anyone who dares to disagree with them? It's like a digital coming-of-age ritual.

But let's not forget the most important rule of all: parents must never, under any circumstances, question their children's chosen identities. Remember, kids are always right, even when they're wrong. It's like a reverse version of the Emperor's New Clothes.

And finally, parents should constantly remind

their children that their worth is determined by the number of likes, followers, and retweets they receive. Because nothing says self-esteem like seeking validation from strangers on the internet.

So there you have it, parents. Your guide to navigating social media and identity development for your children. Just remember, it's all about creating the perfect online persona and never questioning their chosen identities. After all, who needs real-life experiences and personal growth when you can have a perfectly curated Instagram feed?

Now go forth and help your children become the wokest versions of themselves. The world is waiting for their next viral post.

Addressing Bullying and Discrimination in Schools Due to Identity Politics

Ah, the joys of childhood! The innocent laughter, the boundless curiosity, and of course, the relentless bullying and discrimination. Wait, what? Yes, my dear reader, in this age of identity politics, even our little ones are not spared from the clutches of prejudice and intolerance.

Gone are the days when children could simply be children. Now they must navigate a treacherous landscape of microaggressions and trigger warnings. It's like trying to play hopscotch on a minefield. One wrong move and boom! You're canceled.

But fear not, for the enlightened minds of our education system have devised a brilliant solution to address this pressing issue. They call it safe spaces. Yes, because nothing says preparing children for the real world like shielding them from any form of discomfort or disagreement.

In these safe spaces, children can retreat from the horrors of differing opinions and bask in the warm glow of ideological conformity. It's like a utopia where everyone agrees with everyone else and rainbows shoot out of unicorn horns.

But wait a minute! What about the bullies? Shouldn't we be addressing their behavior instead of coddling the victims? Ah, my dear reader, you clearly don't understand the complexities of identity politics. You see, in this brave new world, it's not about right and wrong or good and bad. It's about power dynamics and intersectionality.

So instead of punishing the bullies, we must analyze their privilege and unconscious biases. We must delve into their family backgrounds and examine their social conditioning. And most importantly, we must make them feel guilty for being born with the wrong skin color or gender.

But what about the poor victims? How do we protect them from the relentless torment of their peers? Well, my dear reader, we give them a voice. We teach them to speak up and demand justice. And if that doesn't work, we teach them to cancel their bullies on social media.

Yes, because nothing says solving real-world problems like engaging in online witch hunts and destroying someone's life over a misguided comment or an ill-advised joke. It's like fighting fire with napalm.

But let us not forget the most important aspect of addressing bullying and discrimination in schools: diversity training! Yes, because nothing says promoting inclusivity like forcing children to sit through hours of mind-numbing lectures on privilege and oppression.

We must teach our children that they are not individuals with unique thoughts and experiences. No, they are merely representatives of their respective identity groups. Their worth is not determined by their character or actions, but by the color of their skin or the genitals they possess.

So let us rejoice, my dear reader, for we live in a time where children are no longer burdened with the trivialities of childhood. Instead, they are thrust into a world of identity politics and forced to navigate the treacherous waters of victimhood and guilt. Truly, it is a brave new world indeed.

Promoting Inclusivity and Acceptance in Schools

Ah, inclusivity and acceptance in schools. What a noble goal! Who could possibly be against such a thing? Well, let me tell you, my dear reader, there are some who take this idea to such absurd extremes that it becomes downright comical.

Picture this: a school where everyone is so focused on being inclusive and accepting that they've completely lost touch with reality. Little Timmy wants to identify as a unicorn? Sure, why not! Let's all pretend he has a magical horn growing out of his forehead. And little Susie over there wants to identify as a toaster? Well, let's plug her in and make some toast!

Now, I'm all for embracing diversity and allowing children to explore their identities. But there comes a point where we have to draw the line between acceptance and sheer lunacy. We can't just throw common sense out the window in the name of inclusivity.

But alas, in our current age of identity politics, common sense seems to be in short supply.

Instead, we have schools implementing policies that cater to every whim and fancy of their students. If little Johnny wants to use the girls' bathroom one day and the boys' bathroom the next, well, who are we to say no? Let's just install a revolving door and call it a day!

And let's not forget about the pronoun police. Heaven forbid we accidentally misgender someone and hurt their delicate feelings. We must all walk on eggshells and constantly check our language to ensure we're using the correct pronouns. It's like a never-ending game of linguistic gymnastics.

But here's the thing: by obsessing over pronouns and bending over backwards to accommodate every possible identity, we're actually doing a disservice to the very people we're trying to help. Instead of teaching children resilience and how to navigate the real world, we're coddling them and shielding them from any form of discomfort.

Life is messy, my friends. It's full of challenges and obstacles that can't be solved by simply declaring yourself a unicorn or a toaster. We need to prepare our children for the real world, not create a fantasy land where everyone gets a participation trophy and no one ever has their feelings hurt.

So yes, let's promote inclusivity and acceptance in schools. But let's also remember that there are limits to how far we can take this idea. Let's teach our children empathy and kindness, but let's also teach them critical thinking and resilience. And most importantly, let's not lose sight of the fact that they are children who need guidance and boundaries, not a free pass to live in a world of make-believe.

Chapter 9: The Future of Wokeness

Pushing Back Against the Woke Agenda

Ah, the woke agenda. It's like a never-ending buffet of virtue signaling and moral superiority. But fear not, my dear reader, for there is hope on the horizon. We can push back against this tidal wave of wokeness and reclaim our sanity. How, you ask? Well, let me enlighten you.

First and foremost, we must resist the urge to engage in identity politics ourselves. Yes, I know it's tempting to fight fire with fire, but that only leads to more division and animosity. Instead, let us focus on what unites us rather than what sets us apart.

Next, we must challenge the woke narrative whenever and wherever we can. This means questioning the assumptions and assertions made by the woke brigade. Don't be afraid to ask for evidence or logical reasoning behind their claims. Trust me, they won't like it one bit.

But be warned, my friend. Challenging the woke agenda comes with risks. You may be labeled a bigot or a heretic of social justice. Your reputation may be tarnished and your social media accounts bombarded with angry emojis. But fear not! Stand strong in your convictions and remember that truth is on your side.

Another way to push back against the woke agenda is to support organizations and individuals who are fighting the good fight. Whether it's donating to a free speech advocacy group or sharing thought-provoking articles on social media, every little bit helps. Together, we can create a counter-narrative that challenges the woke orthodoxy.

Lastly, my dear reader, we must not lose hope. The pendulum of public opinion swings back and forth, and eventually, the tide will turn against wokeness. It may take time, but history has shown us that even the most entrenched ideologies can be toppled.

So let us push back against the woke agenda with all our might. Let us challenge their assumptions and assertions. Let us support those who dare to speak out against the prevailing narrative. And let us never lose hope that one day, sanity will prevail.

Building Bridges, Not Walls

Ah, the age-old wisdom of building bridges instead of walls. It's a sentiment that has been echoed throughout history by great minds and mediocre politicians alike. But in the world of wokeness, where identity politics reigns supreme, building bridges seems to be a foreign concept. Instead, we're encouraged to build walls - walls of division, walls of exclusion, and walls of self-righteousness.

You see, in the woke utopia, there are only two types of people: the oppressed and the oppressors. And if you're not part of the oppressed group, well then congratulations! You're automatically an oppressor. It's like a twisted game of identity bingo where everyone loses.

But what if I told you that there is another way? A way to bridge the gap between different identities and find common ground? It may sound crazy, but bear with me for a moment.

Building bridges starts with acknowledging that we are all complex individuals with unique experiences and perspectives. It means recognizing that our identities are not just checkboxes on a form but rich tapestries woven from a multitude of threads.

Take me for example. I'm not just a white, cisgender, heterosexual male. I'm also a lover of cheeseburgers, a mediocre guitar player, and a firm believer that pineapple has no place on pizza. These are the things that make me who I am, not just the labels society has assigned to me.

Now, imagine if we approached others with the same curiosity and openness. Instead of immediately categorizing someone based on their identity, we could engage in meaningful conversations and discover the shared experiences that connect us.

For instance, let's say you meet someone who identifies as a genderqueer vegan. Instead of rolling your eyes and dismissing them as just another special snowflake, why not ask them about their favorite vegan recipes or their thoughts on gender representation in media? You might be surprised to find that you have more in common than you think.

Building bridges also means challenging our own biases and assumptions. It means being willing to listen and learn from others, even if their experiences differ from our own. It's about recognizing that we don't have all the answers and that true progress comes from embracing diversity, not suppressing it.

Of course, building bridges is easier said than done. It requires effort and a willingness to step outside of our comfort zones. But the alternative - a world divided by walls of identity politics - is far bleaker.

So let's put down our metaphorical sledgehammers and start building bridges instead. Let's celebrate our individuality while also finding common ground with those who may seem different from us. And who knows, maybe one day we'll look back and wonder why we ever thought walls were a good idea in the first place.

Embracing Individuality and Unity

Ah, individuality and unity. Two words that seem to contradict each other in the world of identity politics. But fear not, dear reader, for I am here to untangle this web of confusion and show you the path to true enlightenment.

In the wacky world of wokeness, individuality is both celebrated and condemned. On one hand, we are told to embrace our unique identities and express ourselves freely. But on the other hand, we are expected to conform to the ever-changing rules and regulations of identity politics.

It's like being given a box of crayons and told to color outside the lines, but only if those lines align with the approved color palette of the woke elite. Heaven forbid you use a shade that hasn't been deemed politically correct!

But here's the thing: true individuality cannot be confined by the narrow boundaries of identity politics. It is a force that transcends labels and categories. It is the freedom to be who you are without fear of judgment or retribution.

So how do we embrace individuality while also fostering unity? Well, my friend, it starts with recognizing that we are all unique individuals with our own thoughts, beliefs, and experiences. We don't need to fit into a neat little box to be accepted.

Instead of dividing ourselves into endless factions based on race, gender, or any other arbitrary characteristic, let's focus on what unites us. Let's celebrate our shared humanity and the values that bring us together.

Imagine a world where we judge each other not

by the color of our skin or the pronouns we use, but by the content of our character. A world where we can have civil conversations and respectful disagreements without resorting to name-calling and cancel culture.

I know, I know. It sounds like a utopian dream. But hey, a person can dream, can't they?

Now, I'm not saying we should ignore the very real issues of discrimination and inequality that exist in our society. Far from it. But let's address these issues with nuance and empathy, rather than with blanket statements and divisive rhetoric.

And let's not forget that unity doesn't mean conformity. It means finding common ground while still respecting and celebrating our differences. It means recognizing that diversity of thought is just as important as diversity of identity.

So my dear reader, I implore you to embrace your individuality with pride. Be unapologetically yourself and don't let anyone put you in a box.

But also remember that true unity comes from finding common ground and treating others with kindness and respect.

And if all else fails, just remember the wise words of Dr. Seuss: Today you are You, that is truer than true. There is no one alive who is Youer than You.

Now go forth, my friend, and be the best, most individualistic yet unified version of yourself that you can be!

A Call for Common Sense

Ah, common sense. That elusive quality that seems to be in short supply these days. It's like trying to find a unicorn in a sea of rainbow-colored hair and gender-neutral pronouns. But fear not, dear reader, for I am here to bring you a dose of good old-fashioned common sense.

Now, let's start with a simple question: what is common sense? Well, it's the ability to use reason and logic to navigate the world around us. It's the understanding that actions have consequences and that not everything is about our feelings. It's the recognition that we are all individuals with unique experiences and perspectives.

But in the age of wokeness, common sense seems to have taken a backseat to outrage and virtue signaling. We are told that we must prioritize the feelings of others above all else, even if it means sacrificing our own well-being or compromising our principles.

Take, for example, the idea that we should blindly accept and celebrate every aspect of someone's identity. Now, don't get me wrong, I believe in treating everyone with respect and dignity. But does that mean we have to agree with every belief or behavior? Does it mean we can't question or criticize ideas that we find problematic?

Common sense tells us that it's perfectly okay to have different opinions and to engage in civil discourse. It tells us that we can respect someone's right to their own beliefs while still challenging those beliefs. It tells us that we don't have to walk on eggshells or tiptoe around sensitive topics.

But in the world of wokeness, common sense is often labeled as bigotry or hate speech. We are told that if we don't agree with the prevailing narrative, we are part of the problem. We are silenced and shamed into submission.

And let's not forget about the absurdity of identity politics itself. The idea that we should judge people based on their immutable characteristics rather than their individual merits is not only illogical, but it's also deeply divisive.

Common sense tells us that we should judge people based on their character and actions, not on their race, gender, or sexual orientation. It tells us that we should treat everyone as individuals, not as representatives of some larger group.

But in the world of wokeness, common sense is often dismissed as colorblindness or ignorance.

We are told that we must constantly be aware of our own privilege and guilt and that we must constantly atone for the sins of our ancestors.

So what can we do to bring back common sense in this post-wokeness world? Well, for starters, we can start questioning the prevailing narrative and engaging in open and honest dialogue. We can challenge ideas that we find problematic and encourage others to do the same.

We can also prioritize individuality over groupthink. We can celebrate our unique identities and experiences while recognizing that we are all part of a larger human family. We can reject the idea that we must conform to a certain set of beliefs or behaviors in order to be accepted.

And most importantly, we can use our common sense to guide us in our interactions with others. We can treat everyone with respect and dignity, regardless of their beliefs or backgrounds. We can recognize that we are all flawed individuals trying to navigate a complex world.

So let us raise our glasses to common sense, that rare and precious commodity. May it guide us through the murky waters of wokeness and lead us towards a brighter and more rational future.

Creating a Post-Woke Society

Ah, my dear reader, we have reached the final section of this enlightening journey through the treacherous terrain of identity politics. Now, let us turn our attention to the future and ponder the possibility of a post-woke society. Can such a utopia exist? Is it merely a figment of our imagination or a glimmer of hope in this chaotic world?

In order to create a post-woke society, we must first understand what it means to be woke. It is a state of mind where one is hyper-aware of social injustices and constantly on the lookout for any perceived offense. It is a never-ending quest for virtue signaling and moral superiority. But alas, my dear reader, this path leads only to division and resentment.

To create a post-woke society, we must reject the notion that our identities define us. We are not just a collection of labels and categories. We are complex individuals with unique thoughts, ideas, and experiences. We must celebrate our individuality and embrace the diversity that comes with it.

In this post-woke society, we must also reject the idea that certain groups are inherently oppressed or privileged. We must recognize that individuals should be judged on their character and actions rather than their immutable characteristics. It is time to move beyond the victimhood narrative and focus on personal responsibility and accountability.

But how do we bring about this post-woke society, you may ask? Well, my dear reader, it starts with education. We must teach our children to think critically and independently. We must encourage them to question the prevailing narratives and seek out diverse perspectives. Only through a robust education can we hope to break free from the chains of identity politics.

Furthermore, we must foster a culture of open

dialogue and respectful debate. We must create spaces where individuals feel comfortable expressing their opinions without fear of being canceled or ostracized. It is through these conversations that we can challenge our own beliefs and grow as individuals.

In this post-woke society, we must also resist the temptation to silence dissenting voices. We must recognize that true progress comes from engaging with ideas that challenge our own. It is through this intellectual friction that we can refine our own beliefs and find common ground with others.

We must remember the importance of empathy and compassion. In a post-woke society, we must strive to understand and connect with one another on a deeper level. We must recognize that we are all flawed human beings navigating this complex world together.

Let us embark on this journey towards a post-woke society. Let us reject the divisive nature of identity politics and embrace our shared humanity. Together, we can create a world where individuality is celebrated, unity is cherished, and common sense prevails.

Printed in Great Britain
by Amazon

27663150R00086